MW00352203

Additional Praise for *Embedded Finance*

he next phase of insurance is going to see two directions: embedding
urance into real-world services that can be delivered or accessed digi-
y, and incorporating real world services as features or benefits into
rance products. Integrated digital providers have shown the path by
fining industry boundaries and bringing together value propositions
owerful way."

— **Jonathan Larsen**, Chief Innovation Officer, Ping An

tt's and Sophie's combined backgrounds give them a unique per-
e into the future of this space. Their strategic thinking, operational
nce and deep understanding of key players and technologies afford
background knowledge that few people have mastered. If you want to
it, too, read their book."

— **Jelena McWilliams**, Chairman, FDIC

dding is not an incremental step forward, it's actually transforma-
ntually it's going to sound goofy to say you're a fintech company
h a large percentage of all technology companies and brands are
embedded financial services. Getting to know about embedded
must for tech and brand executives, and this book is a good
."

— **Matt Harris**, Partner, Bain Capital Ventures

EMBEDDED FINANCE

SCARLETT SIEBER   SOPHIE GUIBAUD

EMBEDDED FINANCE

WHEN PAYMENTS BECOME AN EXPERIENCE

WILEY

Published by John Wiley & Sons, Inc., Hoboken, New Jersey.
Published simultaneously in Canada.

For general information on our other products and services or for technical support, please contact our Customer Care Department within the United States at (800) 762-2974, outside the United States at (317) 572-3993 or fax (317) 572-4002.

Wiley also publishes its books in a variety of electronic formats. Some content that appears in print may not be available in electronic formats. For more information about Wiley products, visit our web site at www.wiley.com.

Library of Congress Cataloging-in-Publication Data

Names: Sieber, Scarlett, author. | Guibaud, Sophie, author.
Title: Embedded finance : when payments become an experience / Scarlett
   Sieber, Sophie Guibaud.
Description: Hoboken, New Jersey : Wiley, [2022] | Includes index.
Identifiers: LCCN 2022008545 (print) | LCCN 2022008546 (ebook) | ISBN
   9781119891055 (cloth) | ISBN 9781119891079 (adobe pdf) | ISBN
   9781119891062 (epub)
Subjects: LCSH: Financial services industry—Technological innovations. |
   Banks and banking.
Classification: LCC HG173 .S524 2022 (print) | LCC HG173 (ebook) | DDC
   332.1—dc23/eng/20220322
LC record available at https://lccn.loc.gov/2022008545
LC ebook record available at https://lccn.loc.gov/2022008546

Cover Design: Paul McCarthy
Cover Art: © Getty Images | Jose A. Bernat Bacete

SKY10034074_040522

We dedicate this book to the people who have made it possible for two full-time working moms and wives to try to follow their dreams and share their passion with the world. To our husbands, and kids, we love you and we hope we are making you proud. To the rest of you, thanks for your continued support.

CONTENTS

CONTENTS

CHAPTER ONE

THE NEXT FINANCIAL REVOLUTION

G o back for a moment to the early 2000s and imagine hearing about a new phone concept that was going to be more than a phone. In fact, it was actually a mini-computer with most of the screen as glass. That concept would have seemed unbelievable at the time but of course we know now that the concept was the first iPhone. The story we are about to tell about another new concept is as exciting as that and will arguably have an even larger impact. This is the story about embedded finance. It's about a revolution in how people live, interact with, and manage their money.

The early versions of it are already here, whether you realize it or not. Embedded finance is changing how every company in the world, from the largest bank and tech company to the smallest mom and pop shop, does business and how they engage with you.

Part of the history of financial services is the separate but related story of financial technology, popularly known as fintech. Fintech emerged from a crisis in banking and delivered a smoother customer-centric experience with less friction. Have you sent money to a friend via Venmo, Zelle, CashApp, or another app? You were utilizing fintech. Have you used your phone or a tap of your card to pay for your groceries? You were utilizing fintech. What about opening up an account to directly invest in the market yourself through Robinhood, Acorns, or Public? You were utilizing fintech.

How did this technology transform banking, and who were the companies and entrepreneurs to make it happen? How did fintech change consumer expectations, and what impact did this have on banks' strategies? These are all critical questions, because they were the basis of fintech, and fintech is the foundation for embedded finance. Fintech brought banks and technology companies together in order to create new products and serve the digital-centric customer. As we will see throughout this book, embedded finance completes the journey fintech started.

The embedded finance revolution is fundamentally about the seamless movement of money that keeps our society functioning. The friction, the barriers that slow it down, are disappearing. Everyone knows that in most cases, we no longer have to wait in line at a bank branch to complete basic transactions. You can do all (or most of) your transactions from the comfort of your home through your phone or your computer. But it's getting even easier than that. Your money—or rather, your access to your money—is everywhere. It appears when needed at every point of context, instantly and transparently. It's a natural evolution powered by genuine consumer need, enabled by technology. This is a cool concept, but what does this look like in practice?

Today this takes the form of loans at the point of purchase, enabling you to finance a flat tire, or home insurance that appears alongside your new rental agreement. The companies we deal with every day can offer us financial services exactly when we need them, and often we don't need to do anything further, just agree to it. The services, informed by data and powered by machine learning, are optimized for us and are up and running in minutes, sometimes even in seconds.

We call this "embedded finance" because the finance is embedded in another context—a checkout line, a mobile app, etc. From the consumer perspective, it could be summarized as "invisible payments" or "invisible finance," because the key message is that the financial transaction becomes naturally integrated into what you are doing to the point it feels invisible.

Embedded finance is different because it enables companies across industries, with existing audiences, to cater to their customers' financial needs at the point of context. It is an enabler of new revenue streams, stronger customer engagement, and better visibility and access to key pieces of data. Most importantly, it equips technology companies, brands, and retailers with the ability to provide a banking and payments experience to their customers in a seamless, convenient, and authentic way by providing financial services when they need it most, naturally integrated into the experience.

Those of us who have ever gone to a car dealership and explored the option of purchasing a car (new or used) will be familiar with car dealers offering loans on cars. The dealer is not making the loan himself, he is a conduit for the loan, which is made by a bank or a captive finance company affiliated with an automotive manufacturer. The dealership is not offering finance as an act of charity. Without it, the dealer wouldn't make the sale to you, and he earns a percentage of the money you pay for on the loan as well. This works for all sides though, because without the loan, you might not be able to buy the car.

Another classic case of embedded finance in today's world is through Buy Now, Pay Later (BNPL), which happens at the point of sale. You are at an appliance store and want to purchase a $500 TV but only have $200 available to spend. The appliance store, typically backed by a network of partners, will front the money and you, the consumer, have a certain period of time to pay it back.

Buy Now, Pay Later is experiencing a tremendous renaissance today. A recent study from the financial marketplace LendingTree notes that 33% of consumers have tried BNPL and 67% of them plan on continuing to use it.[1] Later in this book, we will explore the reasons behind this trend, and the companies and factors driving it.

WHY NOW?

This book was written to capture a moment in time as well as to serve as a guide to what lies ahead. Whether you operate within financial services, technology, a brand, or business in general, or if you happen to be tech curious, this book is relevant for you because embedded finance is here and only growing and, as with much of life, it is best to be prepared. Embedded finance, by definition, is a global phenomenon and is not limited to any one region or demographic. It touches everyone, which is part of its power. This book tells that story.

It begins with the consumer. She has lived through great financial upheaval, experienced changes in the delivery of services, and is comfortable performing financial transactions digitally. She has a need that a financial product can meet. How does the product get to her? This book tells that story, along with many others. How have her needs and expectations evolved in the digital age? How has the ubiquity of computing power and internet access in the mobile era empowered her? What will her life look like in 2030?

This book will look at all consumers, not just those in the middle class who have the luxury of choosing from financial providers. We will also look at the underserved, the struggling consumer who works multiple jobs and needs innovative financial solutions to make ends meet. For this consumer, investing, and even saving, may be only a dream. How will embedded finance help all consumers live stronger, healthier financial lives?

And while consumers are a crucial part of the story, embedded finance is not only for them, but also for the small businesses. It is for the small businesses who are growing and scaling rapidly, not only the ones who will become the next big IPO, but it is also for the struggling businesses who need a loan to hire that extra pair of hands to take their business to the next level. It is for those small businesses traditionally overlooked by traditional banks but who have great ideas and interesting data points to support a strong probability of success in the future. Those businesses who can utilize embedded finance to make a massive difference in their story.

From an industry perspective, this book provides a glimpse into the future of financial services. The industry is evolving at a rapid pace and while at one time in the past, the bank was the only place you could get a loan or deposit your money, now there are many options. What role will banks, as we know them today, play in the future? How will banks adapt to this new role? Which banks are poised for success and what are the strategies and technologies they have in place to make this happen? We will look at the banks that are embracing the change and thriving, and the banks that are building new products for the new digital age.

WHY US?

Scarlett, the Strategist and Leader, and Sophie, the Entrepreneur and Operator, have been friends for a number of years, sparked by their shared passion around the conversion of technology and financial services. Their combined experience offers a unique, truly global approach to embedded finance. Scarlett has experienced these changes first hand in the boardroom while designing the strategic roadmaps for banks, large and small, on the global level, with a particular focus on the approach to Banking-as-a-Service (BAAS) and the opportunities that lie within. On the other hand, Sophie has spent the last 10 years designing the go-to-market strategy and execution of BAAS providers and more recently, embedded finance propositions across the continent of Europe.

As Jelena McWilliams, the chairman of the FDIC puts it, "Scarlett's and Sophie's combined backgrounds give them a unique perspective into the future of this space. Their strategic thinking, operational excellence and deep understanding of key players and technologies afford them background knowledge that few people have mastered."

With deep expertise in the space, they share a vision and excitement about where and how embedded finance will impact the lives of everyday consumers and the role that Big Tech companies and beyond will have as they become a monumental part of the fintech ecosystem.

After many conversations and many sleepless nights contemplating the vast opportunities, they have agreed that now is the time to tell this story.

WHY YOU?

Whether you're a banker, work at a fintech company, are a business owner, or just a curious consumer excited about the space, we have a lot to share about this new way of connecting consumers with financial services and most importantly, share how your day-to-day life will be impacted for the better.

Banks need to learn to adapt to remain relevant in the new hierarchy. Fintech companies need to shape the financial products that the consumer-facing businesses will ultimately deliver. Once financial services can be delivered through a company or product consumers use every day, there is a tremendous opportunity to reach a greater number of people than ever before, and there is already evidence from early success stories that more progress is possible. We are just at the beginning.

WHAT YOU NEED TO KNOW

The book will provide you everything you need to know about the evolving world of embedded finance from inception to predictions for the future. We will cover:

- **The Early Days**: Proving the historical context and lessons learned from early players and how their efforts shaped the future.
- **The Present**: Identifying the global enablers today, including detailed case studies about their approach with key takeaways you can start enacting immediately as well as highlighting the role that traditional financial service providers continue to play.
- **The Future**: Predicting how the momentum of embedded finance will pick up, what the world of the future will look like, and what the impact on the consumer could be both for individuals as well as society as a whole.

Failing to prepare for, and at minimum be aware of, this monumental shift in how financial products are delivered to customers could lead to serious challenges down the road. The challenges have the ability to impact your talent, revenue, technology you use, and more. This is not the first push toward a new technological world order and we are not far from the days of Kodak failing to seize the digital picture boulevard or Best Buy failing to capture the future of cinematic entertainment. Not everyone should partake in such a journey but, regardless of your ambitions, it is important to understand what is happening at the macroeconomic level as the impact will reverberate into all parts of business. Taking your strategic career hat off and acting as a consumer like everyone else, as a consumer, this book will prepare you for the seismic changes you are about to experience in your day-to-day life.

After all, with a projected \$3.6 trillion global market capitalization by 2030, why wouldn't you want to know more?[2] Let the journey begin.

NOTES

1. https://www.lendingtree.com/tree-news/holiday-shopping-behavior/ Accessed January 25, 2022.
2. https://www.forbes.com/sites/matthewharris/2019/11/22/fintech-the-fourth-platformpart-two/?sh=45ed1e6f5be6 Accessed January 29, 2022.

CHAPTER TWO

THE ORIGINS OF EMBEDDED FINANCE

How big of an opportunity is embedded finance? We will answer this question throughout the book, but before we talk about where we are now and where we are going in the future, we must start with the past.

HOW WE GOT HERE: BANKING IN REVIEW

Let's begin our journey by going back to the beginning of financial technology—**fintech**. Some industry experts say fintech began in the 1950s when the first credit cards were mailed to 60,000 consumers in Fresno, California.

Others point to the widespread adoption of ATMs in the 1970s. Still others look much farther back, all the way to the telegraph system used to transmit financial orders in the nineteenth century.

But the very earliest instance of "financial technology" may be even older than that. Cuneiform is a system of writing developed more than 5,000 years ago in Mesopotamia, what is now Iraq and Kuwait. It was here, and in a few other areas such as Egypt, India, and China, that agriculture developed to a point where dependable harvests could provide food for urban developments, which served as centers of commerce and other forms of specialized labor. On clay tablets unearthed in the Middle East, archeologists have discovered a system of accounting in cuneiform, including loans and credits to farmers for the purchase of seeds, land, and equipment. It may be said without exaggeration that financial services accompanied the very earliest flowering of civilization.

Note that this is well before coins or cash or fiat money. This was an age of barter, of goods themselves being the means of transaction, rather than abstract symbols of value. The first coins seem to have appeared 3,000 years ago in China and a few hundred years later in Turkey. Both were advanced, literate societies with established social norms and laws protecting persons and property. But the act of borrowing and lending is more fundamental to human activity than the idea of "money," as any child on the playground can tell you.

Lending appears to have been a family matter in ancient Mesopotamia, with wealthy families lending from their own reserves. In ancient Greece and Rome, banking became more formal and less personal, with lending and money-changing often tied to the economic activities of powerful entities such as temples or government offices.

The institutions we recognize today as banks originated in Italy during the Middle Ages. Banking groups would finance voyages, gambling that ships would return to port with more valuable cargo than they shipped out. In Renaissance Italy, banking became available to more of the population, what we would today call retail or consumer banking. The word *bank* comes from the Latin *bancus*, meaning bench or table. Bankers (*banchieri*) set up tables outdoors, at the entrance to markets, to help customers solve liquidity problems. They changed currency, operated as pawnbrokers, and made loans to people visiting the market. Wall Street brokers began much the same way, trading securities at tables along the tree-lined streets of lower Manhattan, when commerce was still an out-of-doors activity.

The consumer banking most of us are familiar with arrived in Europe and North America in the nineteenth century, along with industrialization and the emergence of the middle class. And of course, the twentieth century saw the trappings of traditional financial life become standardized: the checkbook, the bills arriving like clockwork every month, the plastic cards, and the bankers in their suits and ties.

Financial services companies have always been one of the most avid and enthusiastic adopters of whatever new technology is available. We already mentioned the telegraph. Banks were also early adopters of computers, the first to bring computing power to their employees—after all, banks have a lot to compute. Today the idea of banks being tech-forward may seem antiquated, because banks typically seem to be behind the times when compared with technology companies, but a look at the technology budgets of the largest banks shows that bankers' enthusiasm for technology remains strong. For example, JP Morgan Chase, the largest retail bank in the US, budgeted an astonishing $12 billion for technology in 2022.[1]

What has changed is that technology is moving more quickly than banks' internal processes, and banks must play catch-up. Mobile technology was taken up enthusiastically in the private world, by consumers, before it saw widespread use cases in business (beyond reaching employees at off-hours). This is in contrast to desktop computers, which first saw adoption in business offices before they became known as "home computers." This gap, along with the stringent regulations banks have followed since the crash of 1929, and later 2008, has created an enormous opportunity for technology companies to enter financial services.

The intersection of banking and technology, or financial technology now commonly known as fintech, began in the internet era. It got its start with digital banking over dial-up internet connections in the 1990s, the arrival of application programming interfaces (APIs) as a communication tool between applications in the 2000s, and truly came into its own in 2009, as the financial crisis wreaked havoc on consumer credit and the entire business of banking. Why was this the moment? The 2009 financial crisis meant that traditional banks became subject to new regulations stemming from repeated crises, and at the same time millions of smartphones (the first iPhone was released in the summer of 2007) found their way into consumers' hands. This created a unique confluence of circumstances for the new wave of fintech companies to emerge and challenge the banks.

Fintech relies on a number of technology layers from a multitude of providers whose interactions can be quite complex, but consumers don't care how all the processes work together on the backend. Very few users know about the financial systems and programming languages used to deliver services to their touchscreens. An important point about fintech is that, whenever possible, it is automated, and performed with minimal human intervention, removing friction as far as possible to complete any desired action. However, when human intervention is needed, fintechs offer this service, and often more seamlessly than the banks because they focus on providing the best possible customer experience.

Though technological innovation is expensive, it is worth the investment, as paying humans to interact with other humans every step of the way (even to check one's balance in a checking account) is even more expensive and does not provide the benefit of scale. The consumer, using sophisticated technology platforms and tools available nowadays, is serving herself and guiding the actions. This means that she should be able to perform the same transaction at 3 AM that she could at 3 PM, and can do it just as well from home or on a train as at the bank branch. She interacts when it is most convenient for her that naturally intertwines with her everyday lifestyle. As we will see, embedded finance takes this key idea even further.

But to return to 2008, financial services in this era still relied on physical locations to deliver products and services to their customers. Branch tellers and their cordoned-off lines were a familiar sight for millions of consumers every day. But bank branches were expensive to maintain, from rent to cleaning to utilities to supplies to employee salaries, and more. To offset these costs, banks had to make revenue elsewhere, like any other business, or think of a way to reduce those costs drastically. The end result of this necessary cost of doing business negatively impacted the customer. Banks retreated from certain products to focus on others, and fintech entered the breach.

One thing that fintechs collectively aren't focusing on is building storefronts. Since 2008, the US has seen a 12% decline in the number of bank branches.[2] In the UK the drop is even more dramatic—a 17% decline since the financial crisis struck in 2008.[3] These declines are to be expected as digital banking is adopted. Indeed, bank branches have been in general decline since the 1980s, as card payments have taken transactions away from cash, and telephone and internet banking offered different means to transfer money. As you might infer from these numbers, digital banks have had more success in the UK than in the US. Particularly for small businesses, digital offerings in the US financial services sector still have a long way to go. Its revenue model is not aligning with customer needs, because banks make money when customers make mistakes. When customers don't pay back their loans on time, or spend more than they have in their accounts, the banks profit. When customers are financially healthy, banks can earn money alongside them, instead of against them.

A word here about the basic revenue model for a bank. Banks earn revenue by providing loans, including home loans (mortgages), auto loans, business loans, and personal loans, including credit cards, and from interchange fees received from card payments. For the privilege of borrowing money, consumers and businesses pay interest. Banks also hold customer deposits, and sometimes charge for this service. These deposits provide the capital to make loans.

Customer needs have changed, and the customer base has grown younger and more diverse. New products and services are required to meet the new customers' needs. Consider how radically other industries have changed over recent decades. It is happening in banking too, but up until now banking has lagged behind the rest of the economy.

CATASTROPHE AS THE MOTHER OF INVENTION

The financial crisis of 2008 resulted from a cascade of causes within the banking industry and in society at large. Loose regulations led to irresponsible lending and borrowing, particularly in the mortgage sector, and then losses from failed loans led to catastrophe for consumers and financial institutions alike. Ivy League graduates formerly flocked to the large investment banks and the secure life they promised, but in 2008 this changed forever. The five largest investment banks at that time were Goldman Sachs, Merrill Lynch, Morgan Stanley, Bear Stearns, and Lehman Brothers. All five were severely compromised by toxic assets (mortgages in default) that were worse than worthless—they were negative equity.

Lehman Brothers went bankrupt in September of 2008, the largest bankruptcy filing in American history, and disappeared. Bear Stearns also failed and was bought for a fraction of its previous value by JP Morgan Chase. Merrill Lynch was similarly acquired by Bank of America. A week after Lehman's collapse, Goldman Sachs and Morgan Stanley announced they would become traditional banks offering deposit services to retail customers. American Express also became a bank around this time. This move afforded the banks more protections by bringing them under closer supervision from federal agencies, which was, for a brief period, an attractive prospect. Japan's MUFG Bank subsequently bought a considerable portion of Morgan Stanley, which also borrowed more than $100 billion from the federal government, more than any other financial institution. Goldman Sachs has since seen considerable success innovating on the retail model with its digital bank, Marcus, named for the company's founder, Marcus Goldman, and more recently with its newly launched transaction banking division and TxB platform, which already supports embedded finance use cases.

The financial crisis resulted in a significant tightening of consumer credit, with some banks pulling back entirely from lending to consumers and small businesses outside of established channels such as credit cards. Just because banks no longer wanted to lend didn't mean that the needs of consumers and small businesses changed. They still needed to borrow money, but the traditional providers were no longer available.

THE TECHNOLOGY THAT MAKES IT POSSIBLE

Smartphones, following the birth of the iPhone in 2007, came of age in the wake of the financial crisis, delivering internet access and computing power to consumers wherever and whenever they wanted it. Apple sold nearly 1.5 billion iPhones in the 2010s, according to company sales figures. Here are a few data points to consider. Nearly all adult Americans (97%) own a mobile phone. Most (85%) of adult Americans own a smartphone, and 62% of them have made a purchase on the device.[4] The average amount of time a person spends interacting with a smartphone is more than three hours per day.

As of May 2021, China counted more than 911 million smartphone users, and India 440 million. The US was next with 270 million users, out of a population of 329 million. One of the marks of a highly developed economy is the percentage of its population that uses a smartphone. The cutoff is generally 70%, though Japan is a notable exception at only 60%.

Deloitte estimated in 2018 that 59% of the global population had used mobile phones for banking needs.[5] This number is likely considerably higher today, especially in response to the pandemic and an acceleration of digital adoption.

As smartphones proliferated in the developed world, feature phones, mobile phones with internet access but lacking the advanced interface of a smartphone, became ubiquitous in the developing world, including the Global South, such as Latin America, Southeast Asia, and Africa. While smartphones allowed consumers in developed nations to avoid the bank branch for everyday issues and to make purchases, feature phones allowed consumers in countries with underdeveloped financial systems and very few bank branches to access financial services for the first time.

Most consumers, some 70%, in Latin America and Africa are underbanked, meaning they lack access to traditional financial services. The transformation of financial services in countries that had underdeveloped banking infrastructure is far more dramatic than the changes happening in countries with advanced banking systems. Smartphone penetration is also expanding rapidly in the Global South, and with it, so are more sophisticated financial services. Brazil counts 110 million smartphone users, and Indonesia,160 million.

One thing we can say is that using mobile phones for finance can be tremendously empowering. With a few clicks, users can see balances, pay bills, and send money to friends and relatives.

Mobile phones open up a whole world to the curious and seekers of knowledge. The potential is endless, though the reality may sometimes fall short. But on a fundamental level, mobile phones opened up rather than closed off humanity, and connected us with every other mobile user.

While much of the focus has centered around mobile phones, the other component to mobile phone success is mobile internet. Mobile internet access has changed the world forever. Mobile, unlike most previous technology, moved from the consumer sphere to the workplace instead of the other way around. Adoption scaled rapidly, we might even say virally, in the consumer world, forcing companies to adopt policies around bringing these powerful devices into the workplace. When we think about the leading indicators that drive the evolving changes in mobile, they lead back to consumer behavior. This behavior not only drives the consumer but also the business world that interacts with consumers. The consumer has never before been as empowered as they are now, and the way they are consuming cultural products such as books (Kindle), movies (Netflix, Hulu), food (Deliveroo, InstaCart, HelloFresh, JustEatsTakeaway), and music (Spotify, Apple Music) is constantly evolving. This has repercussions across their expectations toward other industries, including financial services, as the lines are now blurred on what specific industry offerings look like as consumers want all experiences to be as simple and easy as the last.

The internet provides communication and information tools to the majority of humans on Earth. It has toppled governments, upended industries, and changed the way people live. No business is insulated from its effects. As hard as it may be to believe today, when the internet was young, many experts downplayed its effects and ridiculed it as a toy or fad. Those predictions are laughable now, but underestimating the internet has happened again and again, always with the same result. Embedded finance represents another evolution along this arc.

Many in the banking industry doubted the internet would have much effect on their business. But, like many other industries, it has fundamentally shifted the way that humans interact with the companies they do business with and with each other. The ubiquity of the internet as a truly global platform is a primary reminder that technology and the ability to connect should not be underestimated. Shoppers now search online for deals first even if they intend on making their purchase at a brick-and-mortar store. How many times have you been at an airport, an appliance store, or an electronic store staring at that item that caught your eye to then go online and see how the price compares to a similar shop?

From the youngest to the oldest in society, this has become the norm. As with anything in life, macroeconomic factors from natural disasters, global health crises, etc. change the way that humans operate in their day-to-day life. When applied to the present, the Covid-19 pandemic, and resulting lockdowns, forced many businesses around the world to shift their business model and interact digitally first with their customers. While this had broad scale implications, it was felt strongest with brick-and-mortar shopping experiences and mom and pop businesses. The pandemic caused them to adapt or die and unfortunately, many of them failed as a result of the inability to connect with their customers digitally. The car rental giant Hertz was among these casualties, as were the retailers JC Penney and J Crew.[6] While the pandemic is a deeply timely and personal example for many, it is important to note that there will continue to be large-scale factors that will push consumers online for many of their everyday needs.

Let's now bring this back to the financial services world, one industry that saw both the positive and negative impact of Covid. Those institutions that were already digital first or at least had an adequate digital strategy fared better than those that had digital as a roadmap item that was never quite checked off as complete. Why has this continuously been a theme where banks are slower to adopt change than most, as with the financial crisis of 2008? It goes back to a relatively simple concept: trust. Banks (and other banking institutions such as credit unions, etc.) are the trusted custodians of our financial lives. The financial services industry is conservative with good reason. It is charged with securing the movement and storage of money for both consumers and businesses. It cannot be overemphasized how important a role this is and may be a strong reason why the industry as a whole still uses technology built as long as half a century ago. This has made innovating on time-tested models challenging and expensive. That fact combined with the utter scale that banks had built on the mindset that banks had a monopoly on financial services for consumers. As the world has shifted to external factors, some within the financial industry have tried to get on board by collaborating with startups through acquisitions, investments, innovation labs, and accelerators, but the harsh reality is that large percentages have not. Finding the winning formula can be challenging. In addition to technological challenges, banks are often large organizations with multiple decision-making levels, numerous stakeholders with differing priorities, and departments that often compete for customers. These large ships are difficult to turn, even when the iceberg is clearly visible ahead, but it is possible, as we will see further in the book.

Because of the aforementioned reasons, banks were slow to react to the moment, so when consumers went looking for financial solutions, it was other companies that met their needs.

THE BIRTH OF INSURTECH

According to an article by Jennifer Rudden in Statista,[7] insurance is defined as a contract, represented by a policy, in which an individual or a business entity receives financial protection or reimbursement against possible future losses. Insurance is a concept that most, if not all of us, are familiar with in some aspect of our lives. Whether it be for our homes, our cars, our life, or for specific products, it is a class that we all are used to dealing with and it is one that is in great need of disruption. Today, most insurance policies are sold through existing distribution networks, i.e. the brokers. This means that most insurance policies are still sold offline through a brick-and-mortar office. Florian Graillot, founding partner of the Insurtech investment fund Astorya.vc, believes these numbers to be close to 80% for mortgages and 60% for auto insurance in Europe.

The same way that fintech entered the traditional banking space, insurtech, or insurance technology, entered the insurance space. Insurtech has been around since the early 2010s and the initial cohort of companies in the space focused on B2C, or business-to-consumer opportunities. From the early days in the space, discussions were started around the ability for on-demand or just-in-time insurance. These technologies focused on digitizing the incumbents, the traditional insurance companies, by enabling them to distribute insurance products more quickly. The goal was right but, as we have seen across all industries, the movement to digital can take time and there are a lot of bumps on the road. Close to a decade later, there hasn't been much traction to date as companies discovered that the cycles are incredibly long and the technology stacks of the incumbents were outdated, making it very difficult to plug into the systems. These challenges are very similar to those on the banking side as well. Even if a connection is successfully made to an existing system, the work has just begun. As a result, there are only a handful of players that have managed to truly crack the code.

Of course, as with most rules, there is an exception. One such exception is a company known as Wakam. Formally known as La Parisienne Assurances, Wakam is an example of an incumbent that has seen success in digitizing its services. According to its LinkedIn page,[8] Wakam "is a digital-first insurance company that creates white-label, tailor-made and embedded insurance solutions for its distributor partners and clients via its high-tech Plug & Play platform." Wakam has been in the market for a handful of years and now is one of the most advanced in terms of digitization and its ability to plug into external players. In some cases, Wakam is faster at doing this than the insurtechs that are known to compete with them. What makes Wakam different from the other incumbents who have pursued this path with somewhat limited success? Wakam was able to switch all of its technology infrastructure to API-first, which is game-changing and allows them to do a lot more with third parties faster, in a shorter period of time. As Florian Graillot states, "An insurance company, which is running close to 100% of its activity on the state-of-the-art IT system is quite unique, and I believe that this is the reason why there is an ability to gain market share." As of 2020, according to LinkedIn,[9] Wakam was among one of the top 20 P&C insurers in France.

From those early entrants into insurtech, a few companies are successful, but most are struggling. Because of the struggle, there is a real play for embedded insurance, where we can expect to see adjacent players to the early vision start to push insurance products in the customer journey in a natural way, making it easier for the end customer to understand the value proposition. As Graillot puts it:

> The core value of embedded insurance is education. When it comes to insurance, for most customers, it's a requirement to have insurance policies for your home, your car, and in many countries, your health. Otherwise, it's not really clear why people should pay for an insurance product. By embedding this kind of product in the same journey they are already engaging with makes it obvious, and the value proposition is really clear, which will result in a higher conversion rate.

As we will share many times throughout this book, the focus on an incredible customer experience is absolutely crucial. This may sound like fluff or something easy to do, but it's quite hard to do well. The same issues that arose in banking with the emergence of neobanks and others applies to the insurance space as well. Graillot discussed the importance of the user experience, saying:

> We were running a due diligence on a health insurance startup, and we were having a look at the mobile apps for insurance, and it

was quite surprising because almost all of them, both on iOS and Android, were below three stars out of five. It may appear very easy to achieve a great customer experience but the reality is that it's really tough. We increasingly believe that there is something around the product itself, the user experience that insurtech can deliver at scale and better than the insurance company themselves.

FINTECH RISING

As mentioned earlier, one of the important consequences of the 2008 financial crisis was setting up the conditions for fintech to flourish. Technology companies could now offer services previously only available from regulated financial services entities. The growing use of e-commerce, accelerated by the adoption of mobile internet, increased the need for financial services available literally at consumers' fingertips.

The two areas where new companies first made inroads into banking were payments and lending. PayPal, arguably the first big "fintech" that the world became accustomed to, founded in 1999, was already invading banks' territory by enabling payments online. While there were many other payments startups that have had an impact post-PayPal, the next big shift happened in the mid-2000s with the several new lending startups. Prosper (founded 2005) and Lending Club (2006) were well positioned to take over unsecured personal loans as nearly every bank pulled back from this endeavor that brought much risk and little profit. Banks held back on lending even as economic activity increased post-recession and the demand for loans grew from both small businesses and consumers. Regulations greatly increased on banks, making lending to these customers more complex and technically challenging. Continued low interest rates also made lending less enticing to banks (and saving less enticing to consumers).

Lending Club

Founded: 2006

Market cap: $3 billion

Number of employees: 1,500

Early Approach

Lending Club was founded as a peer-to-peer lending service. Investors would fund loans from borrowers, and Lending Club managed the underwriting and risk. When the credit market collapsed in 2008, Lending Club found itself in demand for personal loans that would otherwise be difficult to obtain as banks were turning away consumers who didn't match their credit profiles. By December 2019, Lending Club had loaned $53.5 billion and was the largest provider of personal loans in the US.

Over time, Lending Club's investor mix moved to institutions rather than individuals, with banks taking the largest role. The company fared poorly after going public, losing 90% of its value in the four years after its IPO, and appeared to have lost its way. Lending Club began as a replacement for banks, then was a vehicle for banks to return to personal lending, and finally became a bank itself. Lending Club bought Boston-based Radius Bank, known for its fintech-forward focus, and now seeks to reverse its fortunes through more traditional avenues.

The phenomenon of new companies, soon to be known as fintechs, taking over individual functions previously only performed by banks became known as the **unbundling** of banks. Banks offer a dizzying array of different products and services. This concept was once a selling point, that an individual or a business could get every product and service related to their financial lives in one place. They were built to be the one-stop shop for your financial needs. Checking and savings accounts, mortgages, credit cards, wealth management and investing—the list goes on, and your local bank can generally do it all. Before fintech, banks competed with other banks on price, and rates, and in some cases geographical convenience, but the products were generally all the same.

The rise of fintech makes sense when you sit back and think about it. How could a single bank with a limited technology budget be expected to create a dozen first-class financial products serving all their customers in a customized way? Add to this that the thousands of community banks in the US lacked—and generally still lack—the technological resources to create top-quality digital products. While they have an abundance of data that should enable them to tailor their offerings, they typically don't have the technology or resources to extract the key pieces of data. Each bank is reinventing the wheel, with thousands of banks each building the same products in parallel and competing with the bank down the street, often while having the same core providers powering them. In general, bank products are generic. You and your neighbor may have very different financial situations, but you are both using the same financial products.

Technology companies operate very differently. These companies are skilled at customizing solutions and offering bespoke options based on the sophisticated use of data about their customers. When this is applied to financial services, the result is an influx of fintech companies specializing in one service that they believe they can do better than anyone else. By offering what they think is a best-in-class product or service, they can own that piece of the pie. This "unbundling" applied to all parts of the eco-system from international transfers (Wise), investing (Nutmeg), to lend-ing (Funding Circle). To start out with, all of these companies focused on delivering a unique and smooth experience for this single service only.

Partner at Bain Capital Ventures, Matt Harris breaks down the evolution of fintech into two components. The first focus is digitization. As Matt puts it, "If you go back 20 years, that's what the world needed. All financial service companies—banks, insurance, and wealth companies—are extremely analog. This is true from account opening through to servicing, underwriting, everything they did required in-presence work and tons of paper." The early fintech companies answered this need. Companies like OnDeck, Lending Club, Square, the first neobanks like Moven and Simple. These early fintechs took well-understood and utilized products and digitized them. While this sounds simple, it is actually quite hard to execute well and the companies that did got big rewards. Many of the companies that were created and grew from the first version of fintech Matt described have gone on to become public companies with valuations in the billions or be acquired for hundreds of millions. There was real traction here, but Matt questions how innovative it was: "It really wasn't changing much about those products other than the user experience. It improved the lives and experiences of consumers and businesses but it wasn't actually fundamentally disruptive."

So what does disruption in financial services look like? That is wave two, according to Matt. In wave two.

> Once you digitize these products, you can embed them in software that consumers and businesses are already using all day. By embedding it, you can make them less expensive and you can inform them with the data that these software products contain. Embedding is not an incremental step forward from that analog to digital phase. It's actually transformative, and we've got room to go here.

A prime example of this in action is through fintech companies like AvidXchange or Bill.com. Their account payable software allows companies to save an incredible amount of time by automating the process, which is a vast improvement from using a lock box operator. As AvidXchange shares on its website,[10] the goal of the software is to "give teams the flexibility, security, and efficiency to approve invoices and make payments anytime, anywhere."

The companies that utilize the data and resources around them to truly understand their customers are the best positioned to offer them financial solutions, which is another point in favor of embedded finance.

With the advent of fintech, banks slowly came to understand they were not only competing with other banks, but with tech-forward upstarts. Soon they would realize there were even more competitors in the market than they dreamed of. If we look at the advantages of technology, data, and a deep understanding of your customer, it is reasonable to think that, at least in part, nearly every company in the world has the potential to be a financial services company!

The new fintech companies focused their efforts on one product, or even one aspect of one product, and devoted their skills and expertise in order to execute it perfectly. With regard to lending in particular, bankers have long argued that Silicon Valley technologists lack the expertise to build the right product and manage the risk, but increasingly these functions are automated and software does the work. As financial services become more digital, technology companies feel more at home with these products.

The first question investors ask entrepreneurs is often, "What problem are you solving?" Fintechs were developed to take on specific problems, such as consolidating credit card debt for which banks no longer delivered solutions. For the generation that came of age in the wake of the financial crisis, there was a feeling that banks were simple utilities rather than companies looking to delight their customers and deliver elegant solutions. And we will see later in the book on why this utility angle, called "banking-as-a-service," is an opportunity banks cannot miss, given the opportunity it represents for them in the era of embedded finance.

Banks foreclosing on the homes of buyers who were encouraged to take out a loan they couldn't afford reinforced this perception. Fintech companies capitalized on this in the early days, emphasizing that banks make money when customers suffer, when they can't pay off their credit card balance every month, or when they overdraft their account. Customers wondered with some justification if their bank was even on their side. This misalignment of interest between banks and their customers led to further alienation and made consumers more likely to seek out nonbank solutions.

This misalignment is not just theory. In 2020, US banks in aggregate collected about $8.8 billion in overdraft fees. This is an unusually low figure from a very unusual year (Figure 2.1). The previous year, banks collected over $12 billion. JP Morgan Chase and Bank of America collect the most in absolute dollars, but overdraft contributes a smaller percentage of their bottom line than regional and midsize institutions.

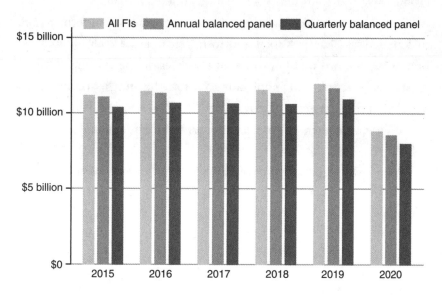

Figure 2.1 Aggregate overdraft/NSF (non-sufficient funds) fee revenues by year in the call reports.

Source: CFPB report Dec. 2021 / Consumer Financial Protection Bureau / Public domain

THE ENTRANCE
OF THE NEOBANKS

The unbundling of the bank continued throughout the 2010s, with virtually every banking function being reproduced and in most cases improved upon by fintech startups. Even backend functions that are remote from the customer experience were re-created by fintech startups.

This continued innovation led to the creation of a new category of fintech called **neobanks**—digital-only banks built from the ground up. Neobanks aimed to take over the customer experience entirely from banks, and offered a broad suite of products for their users, though this range of products was generally narrower than that offered by banks.

The first neobanks launched in the early days of fintech: Simple, co-founded by Shamir Karkal and Josh Reich, and Moven, founded by Brett King, are two well-known retail examples on the US side. Both saw great initial traction, and Simple was known for having the second highest NPS (net promoter score) across all of financial services behind USAA, which serves members of the armed forces and their families.[11]

Simple

Founded: 2009
Market cap: n/a
Number of employees: n/a

Early Approach
Founded by Shamir Karkal and Josh Reich, Simple's mission was to deliver clear and transparent digital banking to a population disillusioned by the financial crisis of 2008–2009. Simple was the paradigm of the neobank in the US.

Simple, which operated completely online, pioneered the Safe to Spend feature and was legendary for its hands-on customer service. The service was bought by the global bank BBVA for $117 million in 2014, and shut down in 2021.

SIMPLE

Shamir Karkal remembers the early days when the idea for Simple emerged:

I was chatting with Josh who was (and still is) a good friend. And he sent me this email saying, "Let's start a retail bank." I remember this was 2009, and we spent a lot of time chatting about the financial crisis and everything that had happened from '07 to '09. It wasn't completely out of the blue for him to talk about entrepreneurial ideas with me, but, starting a retail bank was like, what was out there? He laid out this vision of how customers hated existing banks. The whole financial model of banks was built around trying to sell more products to customers and charge them more fees. What customers wanted had not been articulated, but what customers wanted was financial wellness, and they wanted to have access to their money, and really to live a better life. There was such a deep disconnect between what banks were selling and what customers were asking for. And Josh's idea was, "Hey, let's just build a simple, easy-to-use customer-friendly bank that held your money, helped you pay your bills, gave you loans when you needed them, and then got out of your way and let you live your life." And it was just such a compelling idea. I read that email and I was, like, "Oh man, we should do this now." Facebook and Twitter were already beginning to take off. And yet most banks did not even have a mobile app at that point.

Josh and Shamir launched a website saying, "Hey, we're going to build a better bank. If you like the idea, drop your email and we'll add you to the waiting list." 200,000 people signed up before the company launched a product.

Simple offered a number of innovative features, including displaying a "safe to spend" amount, to help customers stay on budget, and also put a great deal of thought into the customer experience, including customer service, and both Shamir and Josh logged many hours and late nights helping their early customers solve problems. Simple was ultimately sold to the global bank BBVA.

Moven

Founded: 2011
Valuation: $418 million
Number of employees: 49

Early Approach

Banking consultant Brett King launched Moven in 2011 with an emphasis on mobile-first banking. King and Moven were strong advocates for mobile payments, and delivered stickers for customers to use with point-of-sale devices years before iPhones were NFC-capable. Moven's app allowed other banks' card to be linked to it, and delivered more insights and context around those cards and their fees than the issuing banks themselves.

Still privately held, Moven's business focus has moved from consumer-focused to enterprise, and counts several global banks as its customers.

MOVEN

In 2009, Brett King was a consultant and newly minted author of a book about the future of banking called *Bank 2.0*:

> I was on the book tour talking about banking and how it would evolve with technology. I was talking about the fact you'd be able to download your bank account in the future. It'll be embedded in your phone, you'll pay with your phone. It'll give you advice and coach you on money. This is the vision I was talking about associated with my book. And I was speaking to a bunch of VCs from California and they said, "You know, banks aren't going to do this. So who's going to do it?" And I said, "I will." And literally that afternoon, I went home and registered the domain movenbank.com, which became Movenbank, which then would drop the bank and it became Moven. That was August the 18th, 2010. Now, at the time, there was no such word as neobank or challenger bank. Josh and Shamir at Simple and myself, we would often talk on the phone and collaborate because there was just no one else doing this stuff back in the day. And so we called ourselves nonbank banks at that time. And then the term neobank, I think Dave Birch (author and commentator on digital financial services) came up with that one.

King continued:

We were the first mobile direct bank in the world. We were at least the first to offer a debit card from an in-app application for a bank account for Moven. We launched that capability in 2012. We had a bunch of other firsts we did. We were the first mobile banking app that used the home page differently than just listing your accounts.

We put our spending meter and money path on the app, the financial wellness focus. We were the first to do contactless. This was pre-Apple Wallet and Google Pay, so we stuck a contactless sticker on the back of your phone that was RFID-based initially, then there was an NFC tag. We were the first to do a real-time receipt with categorization for your expenses, which we had by 2013. So we really did pioneer the space. But the problem is that we were too early. In 2013, we had a quarter of a million customers in the United States.

King believes that, despite its traction, Moven was too early, but that its features were influential on neobanks that followed, as well as on traditional banks, and remain selling points for Moven's current iteration as a banking-as-a-service tool.

The gap in the market simply was that the bank account would evolve to be contactless, cloud-based, and would coach you on your money. The biggest selling point we used to talk about were things like, you go to a store and you swipe your plastic card, and you don't know what your balance is. You don't know whether the transaction was good or not. The only thing you know is whether the transaction was approved or not. There's not a lot of context in terms of day-to-day spending that will help you make decisions. So now that's how we position Moven and initially the idea was that it would give you smart feedback. If you're getting out of a taxi and you get a receipt on your phone that says, "Hey, you spent $200 on Uber this month" or you come out of Starbucks and it says, "Hey, you spent $400 on dining out and coffee this month" and that elicits behavioral change because most people just simply aren't aware that they spend that sort of money on those activities. So raising the awareness level was a tool to change behavior and make people financially healthier. And that's the way Moven has always worked.

Why did these early neobanks gain traction? They focused on the technology, making it extremely simple to use, and then doubled down on the customer experience. The concept of neobanks wasn't only gaining traction in the US though. Across the pond, neobanks like Fidor, Monzo, Starling and N26 are prominent European examples as well.

Chief research officer at Cornerstone Advisors, Ron Shevlin, known for his contrarian opinions on many subjects, argues that neobanks did not actually gain significant traction compared with bank competitors. Shevlin said:

> I would argue they didn't gain traction, but the gap that they perceived, one perception was right and one was wrong. The wrong perception they had was that consumers didn't want to do business face-to-face, person-to-person. The gap that they were correct in was that there's a way to reduce the cost of the delivery of financial services by not going through the branches.

In other words, digital works, but not because customers don't want to see other humans. Where neobanks succeed, according to Shevlin, is in serving specific niches, such as Aspiration, which serves environmentally conscious customers, or Panacea, which serves physicians starting out in the field.

The neobanks were being formed after years of studying the industry, using contemporary technology and in some cases, operating with updated business models. But neobanks are not necessarily vertically integrated companies that own every piece of the technology stack. They often rely on partnerships with other technology companies that specialize in particular products, and often have banks at the bottom of the stack. Using bank licenses has been an important early step in both Europe and the US. Some of these companies have ultimately gone on to acquire their own banking licenses.

Despite initial traction and a lot of venture funding into the early neobanks, few have gained the traction significant enough to seriously challenge banks, let alone the megabanks with millions of users. The landscape has shifted a bit in recent years and today, neobanks such as Chime (US, valued at $35 billion), NuBank (Brazil, valued at $41.5 billion at the time of their NYSE IPO), Revolut (World, valued at $33 billion), and Tinkoff (Russia, valued at $22.5 billion) are gaining serious traction and, in general, the industry defines them as successful. Each neobank listed above uses varying models to arrive at relatively full feature sets for their customers.

What did those successful neobanks do differently? When asked about NuBank, Chris Skinner, author, commentator and founder of The Finanser blog, believes they have been particularly successful because they reached out for financial inclusion while many banks in the region still do not understand what it means. Financial inclusion in its most simple form is offering banking services to people who cannot afford it. Some 20% of NuBank's customers are individuals who couldn't access banks before. Many neobanks currently try to compete with traditional banks in a similar way. In today's world, the customer needs digital connectivity. Bunq, Starling, and Tinkoff are a few examples of neobanks who understand this concept and are successful in creating digital connectivity to customers who have not been served before.

While, in general, the neobanks have started with one specific product offering, some have done well in expanding their product suites in a compelling way which in turn increases touchpoints with their customers, customer lifetime value, and the total addressable market. This larger movement has become known as the rebundling of the bank and now is being referred to as Super Apps.

What is the difference between the rebundled bank that is digital first versus the traditional players? Customer segmentation. Many neobanks started their journey by catering to specific segments of the population, such as millennials or travelers. Even more specialization is popping up around the globe supporting the theory of specialization and deep knowledge of core customers as a potential winning strategy.

With neobanks' digital-first (or digital-only) offerings, banking services can be delivered à la carte and on-demand, and can happen in any context. Companies, such as Monese for migrants and Daylight for LGBTQ+ consumers, are addressing specific problems for their communities, and building products that make sense.

At the same time, other neobanks who started off with a specialization are now expanding from their initial highly targeted customer base to a much broader one to achieve scale and hit growth targets. Revolut, who initially targeted mostly travelers, broadened their financial services offering beyond multi-currency accounts and cheap FX toward investments, crypto, and savings, and even launched a SME offering, to maintain its growth rate and increase its total addressable market. Tinkoff similarly started off by offering simple credit products before becoming a Super App touching most segments of the Russian population, and plans to expand to the Philippines.

BEHAVIORAL SHIFTS ACROSS GENERATIONS

Embedded finance is an improvement upon fintech, because companies who are already successfully employing embedded finance already start with a significant customer base. Throughout its history, despite all the headlines and money pouring into the space, fintech has struggled with customer acquisition, which represents one of every fintech company's greatest costs. Part of this has to do with low virality of fintech apps compared to social and other types of apps. How many times a day do you scroll your social feeds, whether it be Facebook, Twitter, TikTok, or Snapchat?

What about your banking app? When you do open your banking app, how long are you engaged for? You might tell a friend about a new social network because you want them to join and having them on the platform with you enhances your experience. But, you don't tell your friend about a hot new lending app that will help consolidate your credit card debt, because talking about debt or even wealth can be awkward and uncomfortable and there typically isn't an opportunity for you and your friend to connect and collaborate on the app.

The exception is with peer-to-peer apps, in which you need the person on the other end of the transaction to be part of your network. Another exception is investing and cryptocurrency services, in which people enjoy sharing expertise, and information can be shared without sharing dollar amounts.

There are signs that Gen Z consumers will show greater openness about money and have a greater comfort level sharing personal details, but it is still early in their financial lives. This is certainly true of platforms like TikTok with the craze of "FinTok" and "Finfluencers" including Queenie Tan who, as of January 2022, has nearly 120,000 followers, and Andres Garza, also known as @capital_inteligente, as of January 2022, who has nearly 1,000,000 followers. They openly talk about once taboo topics and make the concepts of financial literacy cool and relatable.

We saw this movement of open sharing for younger generations with the peer-to-peer payments app Venmo, owned by PayPal. Venmo was an early experimenter in making its interactions shareable, encouraging users to invite their friends from other social platforms and making payments fun by adding emojis as descriptions for transactions. It has since made privacy more of a default, but part of the app's original value proposition was showing friends where and how you were spending your money. P2P companies like Venmo are still growing. To quantify the scale of a company like Venmo, Venmo did 2.6 billion transactions worth $159 billion in 2020, 56% higher than the previous year.[12]

Case Study: Tinkoff

Tinkoff Bank's story is unique. It was launched in 2006, before the new wave of neobanks. At the time, founder Oleg Tinkov had spent some time in the US and was amazed by the amount of mail he used to get offering him applications for credit cards. When looking at the number of credit cards per capita, there were two or three credit cards in the US and a fraction of that in Russia. Willing to seize this opportunity, he bought a bank in Russia and launched Tinkoff Bank. The beginnings of Tinkoff were dedicated to selling credit cards by mail, which was a tough process that required important optimizations, including tests of font, signature position, etc., to maximize customer conversions. It created the mindset of test and learn within Tinkoff and laid the basis for continued data analytics within the company. In 2007–2008, the financial crisis hit which led Tinkoff to change its funding model, move most of its activities online, and start taking deposits.

Over the next several years, a growing customer base started demanding more and more services from Tinkoff, which pushed the bank to launch a full product suite, including credit cards, personal loans, point-of-sale loans, and eventually secured products like home equity loans and car loans. On the transactional side, Tinkoff launched a debit card, the largest retail brokerage platform in the market with 70% of all active customers in Russia, and an insurance business focused primarily on car insurance. It also moved into the B2B space through the launch of an SME bank and an acquiring business—Tinkoff is now the second largest online card acquirer in Russia.

Over the years, Tinkoff's data model sophistication improved drastically, catalyzed by the fact that Tinkoff was becoming their customer's primary bank and, as a result, was gathering a very comprehensive data set on their customers, allowing Tinkoff to target those customers with the right product, at the right time, at the right price. Over time, Tinkoff has also added external data sources to its model. According to Neri Tollardo, VP of Strategy of Tinkoff Bank, Tinkoff has now received and processed 250 million credit applications since their launch, which means that most Russians have applied for a Tinkoff product. All that data has gone to enrich their data models, which in turn is becoming more precise and now leverages artificial intelligence to refine its predictions. Tinkoff's philosophy is simple: data is used for the benefit of the customer to make sure Tinkoff can satisfy their financial needs.

When it comes to its target market, Tinkoff's customer base has evolved over time. Tinkoff started by being a regional mass-market credit card lender, outside Russia's big cities, focused on small towns where branches were not always available. The launch of the debit card and the mobile app brought a more mass affluent, younger, and digital customer base, for which Tinkoff developed a certain number of new services. While those customers were not necessarily as interested in credit cards, they wanted to be able to use a brokerage account and buy insurance for their car. Tinkoff also has recently launched a private bank service for high-net-worth individuals. Nowadays, Tinkoff boasts 14 million active customers and covers all segments of the Russian population. Neri Tollardo believes Tinkoff offers a product for everyone.

Tinkoff describes itself as a financial Super App, which is different from China's Super Apps that offer services such as ordering cabs and food delivery. Tinkoff's app offers a single view of all available financial services to the user, whether they are using those services already or not. The idea is to increase cross-selling in a way that is relevant to them. Tinkoff has developed a range of content and materials available in the app, in the form of articles, Instagram-like stories, and tickets, that makes it pleasant for the customer to come back and engage and which ultimately drives cross-selling of Tinkoff's services. Neri Tollardo explains:

> If they are big sport fans, we would tell them there's this football game on this weekend, they can buy game tickets, travel tickets and book hotels. You can do a lot of lifestyle-related activities like book a theater ticket or a sports game ticket all inside the app, which gives the customer an extra reason to come and spend a little bit more time and do something that they have positive feelings about within the app. Obviously, as they do that, it drives the frequency of Tinkoff's app usage.

Tinkoff has also negotiated rates with merchants and is offering cashback to its users. This strategy is most definitely working, as out of its 14 million monthly active users, 5 million of them are daily active users of the Tinkoff app.

We can't discuss customer segmentation excellence and the success that neobanks have had without mentioning that a portion of the traditional finance service players, particularly credit unions, pioneered the customer segmentation piece for financial services.

Many of the innovations commonly attributed to neobanks using advanced technology to segment customers first appeared with credit unions or building societies. Credit unions serve specific groups, for example, the employees of the same business or industry, and therefore were advanced in tailoring their services to meet the needs of their customers, known as members. There are credit unions targeted toward the military, teachers, Disney employees, and the list goes on.

While there are a few primary examples of credit unions leading from a data perspective, such as the early payment of paychecks based on the simple data of direct deposit information, a benefit for consumers that is still a marquee function of neobanks today, there are some differences for this generation of neobanks. The key difference lies in the neobanks' ability to utilize technology and data as a primary competitive advantage. Equipped with this information, the next generation of neobanks allows people of different communities, regardless of location, to become part of the movement.

This customization based on data and truly knowing your customer is where embedded finance comes front and center.

LOOKING ACROSS BORDERS: THE CASE OF CHINA

Yassine Regragui, fintech specialist and expert on China, explains that China's development in fintech is very unique, as it started in 2003, 19 years ago, with Alipay that was an escrow service created to build trust between the buyers and sellers of the e-commerce platform Taobao. Over the years, Alipay became a Super App that is today used by nearly everyone in China. Alipay and its competitor, WeChat Pay, now represent over 90% of mobile payments in China, while their offering extends far beyond financial services into lifestyle. The lifestyle services offered by those payment apps are now used more than 50% of the time by users engaging within the Super App. While this is something very typical to China, we are now seeing similar use cases in Southeast Asia, in Europe, in the US, and in other countries, because these payment apps are expanding their services and taking part in the daily lives of their users. The natural integration of financial services in these Super Apps, along with the fact that Chinese consumers are accustomed to going to one place to meet most of their needs, positions China to be at the forefront of fintech innovation. This is in large part thanks to the Big Tech platforms leading the charge when it comes to financial innovation, a progressive regulator encouraging competition, and the banks that offered API-based services early on to enable Big Tech to connect to it.

China's speed of innovation and technological developments can be attributed to several factors. The first factor is that those who started these payment services are nonbanking companies, including Alibaba, an e-commerce platform and Tencent, a gaming or messaging platform, who built a relationship with their users. Many gamers in the US will be familiar with Tencent for their hit games including Fortnite and PubG. This relationship and Chinese cultural tendency of being more open to new services enable the fast and consistent adoption of the new services they deploy. The second factor focuses on the ecosystem. These two giants have many external services connected to their internal ecosystem (the Super Apps) which creates a halo effect and builds trust externally through their partner's brands. The last factor is the Chinese regulators' openness and support to encourage more competitors to enter to stimulate innovation. By contrast, Western payment companies are kept out of the Chinese market, protecting the homegrown players.

EMBEDDED FINANCE IS HERE

It has taken time for the embedded finance ecosystem to develop. First, banks needed to digitize their offerings and open products and services via APIs, which allow two sites or apps to communicate and exchange data. Next, a sophisticated fintech sector needed to emerge and begin interfacing with bank technology in order to deliver superior versions to their customers, consumer, or business. Third, regulators needed to soften their approach to nonbank vendors offering financial services. Fourth, companies needed to understand the opportunity embedded finance offers and find the right opportunities to offer products. Software-as-a-service companies are seeing the value in financial offerings, which can become the most lucrative parts of their business. Big Tech has the audience, the agility to innovate, and is already searching for solutions to improve customer stickiness and brand loyalty and diversify their revenue base. They also have the data on their users that they can leverage to provide the best possible financial services, at the best price, with the least risk. Finally, most individuals have reached the point of psychological safety needed to start accepting financial services products in other shopping contexts and through different distribution channels.

Embedded finance is officially here. Are you ready?

Summary

Embedded finance is the new way financial services reach customers. Instead of customers going to banks, embedded finance delivers financial products to customers through services they already use, in the context of their everyday lives. Embedded finance was born from fintech, the fusion of financial services and technology that emerged from the financial crisis of 2008.

- Banks have always used technology to deliver services to customers. Embedded finance is the latest stage in this journey, but rather than being the banks themselves distributing the services to customers, banks use tech companies and brands as new distribution channels to reach an even larger number of customers.

- Fintech changed customer expectations of what financial services could be. Fintech prioritized convenience and the user experience, delivered on mobile devices.
- Consumer-facing companies are combining efforts with banks and fintech to deliver financial services in context, at the point of maximum convenience for their customers.

NOTES

1. https://www.ft.com/content/e543adf0-8c62-4a2c-b2d9-01fdb2f595cc Accessed January 15, 2022.
2. https://www.statista.com/statistics/193041/number-of-fdic-insured-us-commercial-bank-branches/ Accessed January 13, 2022.
3. https://researchbriefings.files.parliament.uk/documents/CBP-8570/CBP-8570.pdf Accessed January 13, 2022.
4. https://www.statista.com/statistics/201183/forecast-of-smartphone-penetration-in-the-us/ Accessed January 2, 2022.
5. https://www2.deloitte.com/us/en/insights/industry/financial-services/online-banking-usage-in-mobile-centric-world.html Accessed January 13, 2022.
6. https://www.forbes.com/sites/hanktucker/2020/05/03/coronavirus-bankruptcy-tracker-these-major-companies-are-failing-amid-the-shutdown/?sh=119921dc3425 Accessed January 13, 2022.
7. https://www.statista.com/topics/3382/insurance-market-in-europe/#dossierKeyfigures Accessed January 11, 2022.
8. https://www.linkedin.com/company/wearewakam/about/ Accessed January 13/2022.
9. https://www.linkedin.com/company/wearewakam/about/ Accessed January 13, 2022.
10. https://www.avidxchange.com/ Accessed January 13, 2022.
11. https://www.bain.com/contentassets/7c3b1535c4444f7b8a078c577078a705/bain_report-in_search_of_customers_who_love_their_bank-2018.pdf Accessed January 13, 2022.
12. https://balancingeverything.com/venmo-statistics/ Accessed December 2, 2021.

CHAPTER THREE

BIG TECH AND BEYOND

I n Chapter 2, we explored the history of financial services, which have been intrinsic to society since its earliest days. As technology has advanced, more sophisticated financial systems have been developed to connect with customers. Money has grown increasingly abstract and the customer deals with it at a distance, even invisibly. Embedded finance plays a crucial role as part of this evolution, where financial products are offered in non-financial contexts.

In this chapter, we will explore how technology companies are implementing embedded finance to better serve their customers and the impact it has on the customer and on their business model.

A MATCH MADE IN HEAVEN

Oftentimes, whether it be on the news or through social media, we hear about the Big Tech companies, the companies like Facebook, Amazon, Google, Apple, and others. We call out these four in particular because the total market cap for these four tech giants as of mid-2020 was over $5 trillion and they continue to be four of the five most valuable American companies to trade on public markets.[1] How often do you engage with one of these four players? Our guess is that you engage with a few if not all of them multiple times a day. Big Tech companies have huge audiences and are as much part of our lives as waking up in the morning. It seems that Big Tech has dabbled in just about every market and financial services is no exception. Big Tech companies have been moving into financial services for several decades, but they don't necessarily want to replace banks. And they don't have to. Investors and consumers alike seem to prefer technology companies to banks, so rather than Google calling itself a bank, we have Capital One and many other large banks calling themselves a technology company.

According to a 2019 survey by Bain & Company, accounting for more than 150,000 consumers in nearly 30 countries (Figure 3.1): "54% of respondents trust at least one tech company more than banks in general, and 29% trust at least one tech company more than their own primary bank."[2]

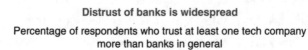

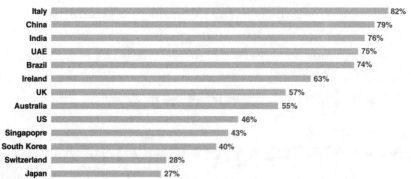

Note: Respondents were asked to rank tech companies (global and local) and banks based on whether they would trust them with their money
Source: Bain/Research Now SSI Retail Banking NPS Survey, 2018

Figure 3.1   Distrust of banks is widespread.

Source: Katrina Cuthell 2019 / Bain & Company, Inc.

Before we look more closely at technology companies and their involvement in financial services, let's take a high-level view at embedded finance and how it is developing today. Embedded finance means that any company can offer financial services to its customers at the moment of need and plays to the strengths of everyone in the value chain. Regulated financial institutions create the basic products (for example, a checking account), fintech intermediaries make those services available via API, or application programming interfaces, which allow the two pieces of software of the fintech intermediaries and consumer-facing tech companies to connect and exchange data, which the consumer-facing tech companies use to deliver the product to customers. The services are offered in context, at the time of purchase as an add-on that makes sense to the customer and naturally integrates into their journey.

Embedded finance makes sense for Big Tech because these companies know their customers, have strong relationships with them, and use their data to predict their needs, offering the right products, at the right price, at the right time. Big Tech excels in areas that make a difference in customers' lives. Apple delivers beautifully designed products. Google provides an array of useful services. Amazon offers a finely crafted customer experience and customer service. Facebook offers connections to friends and loved ones.

As mentioned earlier, the system of payments is one of the first areas that startups and technology companies take on when approaching financial services, and it was also one of the first areas that banks backed out of, because the margins were so low. This is the classic innovator's dilemma case, where steel companies in Europe and the US focused on high-quality, high-margin steel, and ceded low-margin, low-quality steel to small-scale manufacturers in India or elsewhere. But eventually these low-margin manufacturers develop expertise and economies of scale and are in a position to outcompete the established companies.

This is not exactly what happened with banks, but what banks have given up by surrendering payments is data. When other companies manage the customer interactions, they also get access to payments data. When tech companies manage the cash flow of small businesses, they are also in a position to make loans, because they understand how the business works. As Dave Birch, author and commentator on digital financial services, points out, there has been a pivot from owning the account to owning the data. Banks have given up much of the data, and this presents a huge opportunity for embedded finance.

Before the digital era, aside from (perhaps) the government, financial institutions possessed the most complete picture of their customers' lives. When customers took out auto loans, mortgages for homes, or life insurance policies, their banks saw the payments going out, and these were strong indicators of important life events. But today most of these expeditions to find the right product begin on the internet, and a handful of technology companies have the longest and most complete views on customer journeys. It is this data on which the businesses of Google/Alphabet and Facebook/Meta are built. How many times have you gone to search for a gift for your spouse or child to then find that you are shown ads for similar products across your social media? There has been a fundamental shift and financial institutions are not privy to most of this decision-making, especially around the intent to purchase. The digital era has removed financial institutions from their place of prominence in viewing the customer's life events.

MEETING EVERY FINANCIAL NEED

The concept of meeting every need of a customer is a simple one but one that has historically been extremely challenging to execute brilliantly. Through embedded finance, virtually every financial service product can be delivered via API. This includes open banking services and card processing services; payment methods like digital wallets and cross-border payments; traditional banking services, such as checking and savings accounts; lending; and credit scoring. Let's look at a handful of these products in more detail.

Digital Wallets

Digital wallets are pieces of software that store payment credentials, most commonly payment cards. Apple Pay, which is part of the iPhone operating system, and the app-based Google Pay, are prominent digital wallets. Both are examples of financial products built by technology companies on top of traditional financial services rails. Google Pay uses the Wise API to offer international payments to its users. Wise, formerly known as Transferwise, is a leader in low-friction international money transfers.

Apple Pay and Google Pay are examples of tech companies using embedded finance to offer better experiences for their customers at the POS, or point of sale. Why pull out a flip-open wallet from your pocket and then a credit card and insert or swipe when you can simply tap your phone and pay for the purchase instantaneously? How many times have you gone to pay for something at a gas station or grocery store only to realize you left your wallet at home? With digital wallets, all you need is your phone or smart watch, both of which are usually attached to people these days. Digital wallets can be more than just replacements for physical wallets. They can be gateways to a huge array of financial services from multiple providers. Expect digital wallets to take on larger roles in all our financial lives in coming years.

Savings Accounts

Savings accounts are seen as nice to have, not as a must-have, primarily because savings haven't been prioritized from a financial literacy perspective and many people don't have the knowledge or, in many cases, the ability to save meaningful amounts. On top of that, many of those who have attempted to save in a traditional savings account often get frustrated at the low interest rate they receive on their account; at that rate, some feel their money is better kept in a jar on their dresser.

This mentality is shifting though, especially with Gen Z, who as a group are anxiously looking for ways to save, responding to the challenges of their predecessors. Naturally, companies that facilitate savings will be seen as valuable to demographic groups like Gen Z. A 2018 study by the National Society of High School Scholars reports that nearly half of young people hope to start saving in their twenties, ideally sooner.[3]

A savings account, whether for health reasons, education, or retirement, is a powerful incentive to enhance brand loyalty in the long term and companies now have the ability to establish that relationship when a purchase is made. Imagine the ability to better the lives of your customers by helping them build their wealth in a way that is naturally integrated into their daily lives. This is already happening within financial services with banks like Bank of America, which provides the ability to round up your change on every purchase you make and put that money into your savings account. This concept is starting to gain traction and the savings-as-a-service fintech Raisin is one of the standouts in this field, although most of their partnerships currently are with banks and neobanks, but there is little doubt the embedded finance use cases will pop up soon.[4]

International Cross-Border Payments

Cross-border payments have been a longstanding pain point for customers who work outside their home countries or have family abroad. Traditional banking services such as wire transfers are a cumbersome and expensive process and have changed little in recent decades. Users of apps such as WeChat (owned by the Chinese company Tencent), Remitly, and

Worldremit, can send money quickly and inexpensively across international borders. Flywire helps students paying tuition abroad to make payments. The company also serves patients receiving treatment in other countries. Flywire works with more than 2,000 companies around the world, helping them receive payments. They form strong relationships with payees and those paying them alike.

Lending and Buy Now, Pay Later

Along with holding funds, lending is a fundamental aspect of financial services. Today, the greatest advancement in lending and credit is occurring in Buy Now, Pay Later (BNPL) financing at the point of purchase. BNPL may be available to customers unable to procure other forms of credit. It helps form a bond between the retailer and the buyer, and also helps merchants avoid fees charged by payment networks. In the online world, it dramatically lowers cart abandonment, and leads to increased sales. We will have a great deal more to say about BNPL in Chapter 4, which focuses on brick-and-mortar non-tech businesses.

BIG TECH IS PART OF CUSTOMERS' EVERYDAY LIVES

By now most of us are accustomed to seeing recommendations on Amazon or Netflix that seem to indicate the services know us better than we know ourselves. We are used to seeing marketing on Facebook that makes it seem like Mark Zuckerberg has been listening to the conversation we just had with our spouse about a trip to the Caribbean only to find ads for hotels in the Bahamas on our next log in.

The tech giants know us, for better or worse, and because of their transactional nature, each of these companies is already deeply involved in the world of payments, traditionally the domain of banks, and they are increasingly part of the lending and credit landscape as well. But embedded finance means tech companies can assume an even larger role in customers' lives and earn money and customer loyalty by doing so.

Let's talk about the loyalty piece for a moment. To this point, we have continuously emphasized the importance of experiences and meeting customers where they are, but let's explore another side of this, loyalty and brand affinity. Remember when the iPhone and subsequent versions launched? People were rushing to YouTube and other streaming channels to watch people unbox the devices—it was a collective moment in time.

For those who have iPhones, do you remember your first iPhone and how it felt to open that box for the first time? The design and wrapping were done in a way that was very Apple and you felt part of a club. This passion for brand is not only true for electronic devices, but across retail as well. Nike is famous for their unboxing of limited edition sneakers with no attention to detail being overlooked. Each part of the unboxing has a story and a moment within it. This connectedness and true brand affinity differentiate these iconic brands from traditional financial services. That feeling that was just described with the unboxing of the iPhone above, have you ever had a similar feeling opening up your first bank account or receiving a new credit card?

It has been mentioned that there is little incentive for tech companies to become banks, which would sink them into a world of regulations and capital requirements, so why would they want to be involved in embedded finance? For the revenues, of course, but also for increasing customer loyalty and ultimately lifetime value. Companies actively participating in embedded finance are predicted to reach a market capitalization of $7 trillion by 2030, making it a very attractive business to get into.[5]

But why should customers entrust their financial lives to technology companies rather than the traditional players in the space, the banks? As the data in Figure 3.1 showed, most customers have a less problematic relationship with technology vendors than banks. Our relationship with money is a complicated one, and if the only experience you have with your finances is to spend money and then check your balance or get notified of fees, it makes sense that you would not have the warmest feelings toward your bank. Technology companies offer much more diverse experiences, and money is secondary. It is possible to cruise around Amazon for hours, reading reviews and discovering new products, without buying a thing. But when it comes time to buy, we feel very informed about our purchases.

It's also worth remembering that the Big Tech companies have a history of financial innovation. Mobile payments are now an everyday feature in the lives of millions of consumers. The most common services used today were pioneered through partnerships spanning the entire payments ecosystem, and delivered to customers not by the big banks but by Apple, Google, and Samsung.

Technology companies may not be perfect, and some of them indeed have a history of troubling behavior regarding privacy and customer data, but the majority of consumers care less about these details than governments do, as evidenced by their willingness to voluntarily share their data. Tech companies manage to keep their often huge pool of customers satisfied, and they're good at selling. Not only do people trust tech companies more than their banks but they trust the tech companies to offer financial services. McKinsey found in 2019 that 58% of customers said they would trust Google to provide them with financial services.[6] This is not surprising. Google, like the other tech giants, has a loyal following and a strong brand, being nearly ubiquitous in the online experience of billions of users. And it is not just consumers. Investors are also betting on tech, and why not? Very few people think technology companies are due to shrink or lose market share in the near future, except in highly specific contexts, such as countries barring them from operating, or regulators interfering with their operations. In the same McKinsey report, it was found that in 2020 the market capitalization for the seven largest technology companies exceeded $8 trillion, almost double that of the top 200 banks in the US.

This disparity in valuations is at least partially due to technology companies beginning to offer financial services, according to the McKinsey report. Technology companies are also seen as more resilient to economic crises.

Embedded finance provides wholly new experiences for customers, removing the historically cumbersome checkout payment experience entirely, as with Uber rides and deliveries where customers don't have to pull out their wallet while getting out of the car at the airport or when their food is delivered to their front door. Technology companies invest in creating superior user experiences, to the point of removing "banking" from the process entirely.

Because Big Tech enjoys overwhelmingly positive customer sentiment, companies have the opportunity to meet and exceed their customer expectations to further increase their brand loyalty. One of the things that Big Tech has proven to be good at is anticipating customer needs. Apple proved that, though the customer may always be right, sometimes they must be strongly guided to give up things they previously thought essential, such as floppy drives, USB ports, and headphone jacks. Big Tech gives customers what they want, and in this case what customers are asking for is financial services, whether or not they are classifying it as such.

The maturation of fintech offerings, from neobanks to digital subscriptions, means modern customers are increasingly habituated to getting their financial services needs met outside their traditional bank. They can now access financial services at the point of use, without having to think about it or having to go somewhere else. They want the convenience and the relevance of being offered the right financial service at the right time, based on the data shared with their favorite brands. Data shows time and time again that consumers will welcome increased interaction with their preferred brands if it is relevant and helpful. Every company must ask itself, after studying the data, do you really know what your customer wants, and are you prepared to deliver it in a way that is beneficial to them?

Look at Apple's forays into financial service in the last decade. Apple allows payment at the point of sale and online with the click of a button because its Apple Pay system is embedded in the iOS operating system. Apple leveraged Apple Pay into the Apple Card, offered in partnership with Mastercard and Goldman Sachs. Although Apple is a manufacturer of hardware and software, its services, including its payment and card services, form an ever-larger part of its revenue mix. Apple's services revenue grew 25% in 2021 over 2020.[7] Apple's payment functionality is easy to embed in new iOS apps made by third parties, since it is native to the operating system.

Google and Amazon offer similar payment functionality, though each has different areas of strength and customer penetration. But are the large technology companies exceptions rather than the rule? How do other companies without these structural advantages participate?

BEYOND GOOGLE, APPLE, FACEBOOK, AND AMAZON

We've been speaking primarily about the very largest technology companies so far, but embedded finance is not limited to companies with vast budgets and hundreds of millions of users. Any company with customers that trust them and that has a product customers want to buy can also offer financial services. We will talk more about how, what this looks like, and models for success throughout this book.

Uber

The rideshare company Uber was notable early on for making payments invisible. Once a card was loaded into the app, users could summon rides and go on their way without touching their money (or looking at the price!). This payment experience will become increasingly common across many areas of our lives, as we will discuss later, but Uber is interesting for another reason.

Gig economy companies such as Uber have a special opportunity. They employ large numbers of drivers and delivery people who work on demand, their services called upon with a tap of a mobile screen. These workers do not have traditional employment relationships, and often do not carry health insurance or enjoy other protections that more traditional workers enjoy. They often lack access to credit. Recognizing this, Uber was one of the first companies to offer banking services to its employees through its app. Uber drivers and gig economy workers generally might otherwise struggle to obtain these services, because of their nontraditional pay and often precarious financial situations.

It is no exaggeration to say that the banking services offered by mobility and delivery companies provide a lifeline to workers and their families. Some drivers need to cash out at the end of every day to buy fuel or care for their vehicles or pay time-sensitive bills for their families. With visibility into earnings, it should also be possible to offer loans to drivers, even those with limited or nonexistent credit history. Indeed, this is already happening in Mexico, where the global bank BBVA is offering credit to Uber drivers.

Grab

Asia-based transportation and food delivery giant Grab, who acquired Uber's Asian operations in 2018, and with a presence in eight countries in Asia, offers a full range of financial services to their drivers, merchants, and users, ranging from payments, to insurance, lending, and wealth management. This approach has made them one of the most successful Super Apps in Asia, with a growth of their financial services total payments volumes reaching a compound annual growth rate (CAGR) of 102% between 2018 and 2020 from $2.2 billion to $8.9 billion and revenues increasing from $90 million to $342 billion over the same period.[8] The fact that Grab has applied for a full digital banking license, together with Singtel in Singapore, demonstrates how big their plans are when it comes to financial services. There is no reason for this model not to grow. Every group of customers not served by a traditional incumbent presents an opportunity for a challenger. Technology allows rapid iteration of products and inexpensive distribution to target highly segmented groups.

Case Study: Shopify

Similarly, the e-commerce platform Shopify, which began by offering shopping cart functionality to online merchants, has expanded its operations into areas typically served by traditional financial institutions. The company knows its sellers' businesses and cash flows, which makes it easier to understand and offer access to financial solutions for independent businesses that are underserved by existing financial products. Shopify's offerings remove the barriers to entrepreneurship and business growth. In fact, for every $1 of Shopify revenue, their merchants generate $40.82, as reported in the 2021 economic impact report.[9]

The origin story of Shopify is like so many we have seen. Back in the late 2000s, Shopify founder and CEO, Tobias Lütke, better known as Tobi, was trying to start a snowboard company on the internet and realized how much friction there was and how difficult that was to do, especially the process of setting up payments. What Tobi and the team discovered was that there were financial tools for independent businesses that weren't being met by the big banks or financial institutions. Specifically, big banks didn't want to work with entrepreneurs and independent businesses, they were risky and many of them failed, making them a challenging investment case. Shopify saw this as an opportunity to build relationships with entrepreneurs of all kinds. They have an entrepreneur-first mentality and like to refer to their work as "Arming the rebels," the creators and makers of the world, to help push their ideas and products forward. When asked about key factors in Shopify's success, Tui Allen, product director at Shopify, spoke about the importance of knowing your core competency. For Shopify, that centers around the merchant and what it takes to make an entrepreneur successful. Given the complex nature of being a business owner, Shopify spends a tremendous amount of energy focusing on the experience. Most specifically, as we have seen with other large tech players to this point, Shopify makes the user experience and design incredibly simple to encourage broad adoption and continued usage.

When asked about Shopify's strategy related to embedded finance, their approach is focused on the "win-win-win" model. As Tui shared:

> I think finding the right win, win, win commercial and economic model is really important when you're bringing embedded financial solutions to market. How do I bring something and provide value to my customers? And how does that value then ultimately also provide value to their customer? And how do we ensure value for our partners (if we have one)?

In terms of the types of partnerships where this win-win-win model works well, Shopify has found great success with the likes of their partnership with Affirm and Stripe within the fintech landscape and outside-of-the-box partnerships, like the one they have with social media platforms like Pinterest, TikTok, and more.

When asked about Shopify's view on the importance of embedded finance for the future of the business, Tui said: "Embedded finance is in our DNA. It is core to our entire strategy. We anticipate that embedded finances are going to continue to grow as we remove more of those financial barriers and those friction points that still exist for independent entrepreneurs across the world." A strong statement in support for the future of embedded finance. Removing the friction points is crucial in the goal of allowing businesses of all stages to "reinvent what they do and do it in a way that is fast, easy and simple."

So what do the numbers say about Shopify's growth? As of October 2021, in Q3 Shopify had $20.5 billion in gross merchandise value, also known as GMV, processed on Shopify payments. This number was up 49% versus the same quarter the year before. For Shopify Capital, their business unit offering funding for businesses using their platform, as of October 2021 and since its inception in 2016, merchants have received $2.7 billion in funding across the US, Canada, and the UK.

This is just the beginning for Shopify. Based on the traction and growth Shopify has seen to date, they are incredibly well positioned to be a prominent player in embedded finance moving forward. With the aforementioned new partnerships with the likes of Affirm and Stripe in the US, they will be getting more heavily into Buy Now, Pay Later services as well as offering a new money management account, Shopify Balance, with the vision of being the "central hub for managing your finances on the Shopify platform, moving from just running your shop or store, to running your entire business on Shopify," according to Tui. This future look is so much more than just financial services, it applies to all aspects of running a business, from shipping and fulfilling, to the point of sale systems if your business is a brick-and-mortar one.

BENEFITTING THE END CUSTOMER

Much like the "win-win-win" philosophy that Tui shared, Marqeta CEO and founder, Jason Gardner discussed his strategy for successful partnerships:

> We think about it as a network of networks where we benefit because those cards are being built and deployed on Marqeta's platform, we help our customers grow, which they see a direct benefit of that and we see a benefit because it helps our platform grow.
>
> Anything that can dramatically improve the experience for the end customer will gain the most traction. Oftentimes within financial services, there is a tendency to focus on the transaction, but if we shift the thinking to the desire or the event, the process changes. The event is ordering the Uber, the payment is invisible and happens in the background. If you order food off of Grubhub, you focus on what you will eat, when it will arrive, and the payment becomes secondary.

Jason believes that every large tech company will eventually want to become a payments company. Why would this be the case? The reason is actually quite simple: banks have large constituencies that they know a lot about, and many of these constituencies have had the same bank account for a decade plus. As Jason says, "Money creates loyalty. To create loyalty, it makes a lot of sense to embed banking services within their constituency. Shopify and Grab are great examples of companies doing this well." Providing the value proposition to your customers in a way in which they get something in return for it is a significant thing. There are many ways to define what that value looks like. One way is through speed. With the Square Card, people get their money faster. Through Bill.com, businesses are able to pay their bills faster, helping their business grow more quickly.

THE CASE FOR E-COMMERCE

Big Tech has led the way in embedded finance, but many smaller technology companies are beginning to follow these examples. Carvana is an online marketplace that sells second-hand automobiles. It is famous for its "car vending machines" that stand several stories tall—more memorable marketing than a billboard and communicating the brand's core message of making car-buying easy and unintimidating. Carvana is a software company that sells cars, but it also sells financing on the vehicles it sells, as well as insurance options. The sale of each vehicle may not bring much money (though the margin on used cars is significantly higher than on new cars, and used-car prices stood at record highs as this book was being published) but financing and insurance cost little to add on and may bring in meaningful revenue while also being convenient to the customer and forging stronger bonds with them for a continuing relationship.

Similar opportunities are offered by e-commerce platforms that serve multiple sellers. Those that serve sellers help them get business done without worrying about regulations or paying high banking fees to accept payments and send disbursements. This is a virtuous cycle, helping e-commerce platforms attract more customers while serving them better. One example of this concept playing out is Salesforce. Salesforce's core offering is customer relationship management (CRM) software. Its product is its software, making it a software-as-a-service (SaaS) provider, and it is known as a horizontal rather than vertical SaaS company because it serves many industries, not just one. But through its Commerce Cloud offering, an e-commerce platform, Salesforce is also an e-commerce company. It can provide not only marketing and inventory management, but also accounting software and payment processing. Accounting is another launching point for embedded finance. The accounting software provider Xero manages the business data of its customers, and this integration makes it perfectly placed to offer business loans, which it does in Australia and the UK.

Amazon, the paradigm of online marketplaces, has spawned imitators around the globe. Each region of the world faces distinct challenges, and companies must come up with creative solutions to capture market share and meet customers' needs. Many regions of the world have faced chronic shortages in financial services and lack financial instruments such as credit ratings to determine the likelihood of borrowers repaying loans. This presents a huge opportunity to fill this gap for both businesses and consumers by businesses that have relationships with these types of customers.

Nigeria-based Jumia is a marketplace of goods and services that is sometimes called the Amazon of Africa. Because it hosts multiple sellers and understands their businesses, it can offer lending services to those sellers. These data-rich relationships enable highly efficient underwriting. The sellers can do more business, which in turn benefits Jumia. Marketplaces can even offer full-fledged banking services, enabling sellers to borrow money in order to stock up before the holiday rush, enabling more sales. Offering Buy Now, Pay Later options to sellers' customers at the point of sale is also a revenue boost and is a perk that is being offered more and more across geographies.

Another industry that has seen strong traction around embedded finance over the past few years is cryptocurrency exchanges. (Cryptocurrencies are digital currencies whose transactions are run by decentralized systems relying on cryptography, rather than governments or central banks.) Some of those platforms started by providing existing cryptocurrency holders the ability to exchange coins on their platform for other cryptocurrencies held in separate wallets.

Bitstamp, one of the leading crypto exchanges in the world, very early on spotted the advantage of adding the capability of fiat deposit and withdrawal by their users to their platform. Bitstamp was launched in 2011 by its two founders, Nejc Kodrič and Damijan Merlak, after they realized the massive opportunity arising from the fact that to buy cryptocurrencies at the time it was necessary to send money to Japan, and purchases took three to five days. They decided to launch a crypto exchange in Europe, where the European clients could buy crypto very rapidly by giving them the ability to make fiat transfers to the bank accounts of European banking partners. Jean-Baptiste Graf.tieaux, CEO Europe of Bitstamp, believes that is the reason why they are now one of the platforms with the strongest network of banking partners as they invested very early on in building those relationships and capabilities for their users.

In an effort to seize the opportunity of more volume that the democratization of cryptocurrency trading would bring, many exchanges have added the ability to come with no coin and buy them directly onto their own platform, shifting the model of the separation of crypto exchanges and crypto wallets to a more integrated one with a one-stop-shop offering. Coinbase's mission is to "create an open financial system for the world" and in that context, beyond the simple purchase and sale of cryptocurrencies, has started offering the ability to save and borrow against one's crypto assets.[10]

Marqeta CEO Jason Gardner sees a tremendous amount of value in exchanges. Outside of the partnership with Coinbase, they have also partnered with Bakkt and Shakepay. Today, it is still challenging to convert crypto. The easiest way to do it is through your card where you are able to spend your crypto at whatever shop or restaurant you want. To help solve this challenge, Marqeta created a gateway with Coinbase so that people who hold different forms of crypto in their accounts can connect a card to their Coinbase wallet and make purchases at the point of sale. The transactions are funded in fiat currency at the prevailing dollar price in real time. The cards work both online and offline and allow people to find value in their crypto beyond converting it to fiat currency. The end user can use the card as if it were any debit, credit, or prepaid card.

While a few of the cryptocurrency platforms have also taken the leap of self-regulation, such as Coinbase, Bitstamp, and Kraken, those platforms rely on banking-as-a-service providers such as Clearbank or Fiat Republic to enable those on- and off-ramp fiat flows to ease their user journey in the world of cryptocurrencies.

The arrival of the Metaverse, immersive virtual worlds incorporating virtual reality and using a blockchain infrastructure, with players such as Meta (formerly known as Facebook), the Sandbox and Decentraland, will further accelerate this trend of the intersection between fiat and crypto-currencies and eventually, embedded finance in those immersive worlds.[11] Many opportunities for real-world players will stem from it as we can see already with the opening of the first H&M shop in CEEK city,[12] the acquisition of the virtual shoe company making non-fungible tokens (NFTs) and sneakers for the metaverse RTFKT by Nike,[13] or the launch of Adidas's Into the Metaverse NFTs that minted in a matter of hours.[14] We will see more about this upcoming trend later in the book.

The business cases may be very different, but in all these examples, sellers are layering financial products and services on top of non-financial products and services to deliver deeper value to their customers in the time and place where it is needed.

WHY EMBEDDED FINANCE MAKES SENSE FOR BIG TECH

As a brand or tech company that engages in embedded finance, when more and more of your primary revenue comes from financial services through things like payments, lending, and insurance, the software portion of your revenue actually becomes less important. Why does this matter? According to the Software Products Global Market Report 2021, the total addressable market for global software products was $930 billion in 2020.[15] According to the Business Research Company's Financial Services Global Market Report for 2021, the global financial services market size was $20.4 trillion in 2020.[16] That is a market size 20x the size of software companies. The market opportunity is enormous. Building out the embedded finance part of your business, therefore, is a huge differentiator, because now you can get creative around your pricing models in ways that your competitors can't. Potentially removing the cost for the software portion of your offering can quickly result in greater customer acquisition, which in turn allows you to offer more embedded finance products, giving you more data on more customers and greater revenue and the cycle continues from there.

Big Tech is already layering financial products on top of its core offerings, and this will only increase. Even Apple, the most profitable consumer-facing company in the world, has benefited immensely from financial services. The largest technology firms are well positioned to profit from embedding financial services in their user experiences. They enjoy massive customer bases, positive consumer sentiment, large budgets and skilled product teams, and can roll out products rapidly, skillfully, and at scale.

Most companies do not enjoy all these advantages, but they can still participate in the embedded finance revolution, and indeed it would be a missed opportunity not to get involved. And those that get in early have an advantage. Embedded finance is here and only growing. As Matt Harris, partner at Bain Capital Ventures, puts it:

> For software companies facing off against retailers broadly defined, whether it's a Shopify merchant or WalMart, they will be majority financial services in five years, for sure. No question. It will be slower in other verticals where the payments acceptance wedge is less prominent, but, as B2B payments get more and more digital and therefore monetizable, I think it'll get close to 50 percent in every vertical.

Ron Shevlin, chief research officer at Cornerstone Advisors, points out that embedded finance, while it can deliver revenue and advantages over the competition, can also be viewed as another way for companies to make life more convenient for their customers. "This is not about companies trying to become financial services providers," Shevlin said. "They're trying to find ways to add more convenience to their customers' lives, simplify the financial transactions and generate and create more loyalty among their customer base."

Technology companies already know their customers and have data on their needs. They have product teams that can build quickly. Fintech companies and certain digital-forward banks have built out the infrastructure to plug into tech companies' front ends and are eager to partner on solutions. Several successful implementations have been described in this chapter. What other companies will join them in the months and years to come?

Chapter 4 will examine the growth of embedded finance offerings in the offline, or brick-and-mortar world where the bulk of spending still takes place. Traditional points of sale present different challenges to offering financial services, but with hybrid online-offline offerings, powerful opportunities are available to retailers and brands that can craft the right experience for their customers.

Summary

Technology companies have changed customer expectations in recent years. Consumers interact with tech companies multiple times every day. Customer journeys begin with the technology companies, so it makes sense that they should also be delivery vehicles for financial services.

- Tech companies are already innovating in financial services, particularly in the area of mobile payments and lending.
- Tech companies have the most complete view of a customer's behavior and can use this data to offer financial services at the right time, place, and price.
- Companies like Shopify and Grab have seamlessly moved into financial services, making it a substantial part of their business. There are vast opportunities for others to do the same.

NOTES

1. https://www.axios.com/big-techs-power-in-4-numbers-de8a5bc3-65b6-4064-a7cb-3466c68b2ea0.html Accessed January 14, 2022.
2. https://www.bain.com/insights/many-consumers-trust-technology-companies-more-than-banks-snap-chart/ Accessed January 14, 2022.
3. https://www.nshss.org/lp/2018-career-interest-survey/ Accessed January 13, 2022.
4. https://www.raisin.com/press/ Accessed January 2, 2022.
5. https://www.simon-torrance.com/blog/EmbeddedFinance1 Accessed January 14, 2022.
6. https://www.mckinsey.com/~/media/McKinsey/Industries/Financial%20Services/Our%20Insights/Inflection%20point%20Seven%20

transformative%20shifts%20in%20US%20retail%20banking/Inflection-point-Seven-transformative-shifts-in-US-retail-banking-vF Accessed January 14, 2022.

7. https://www.macrumors.com/2021/10/28/apple-services-revenue-q4-2021/ Accessed January 14, 2022.

8. https://assets.grab.com/wp-content/uploads/media/ir/investor-presentation.pdf Accessed January 2, 2022.

9. https://news.shopify.com/the-shopify-effect-36m-jobs-and-307b-in-economic-impact-in-2020 Accessed January 30, 2022.

10. https:/www.coinbase.com/mission Accessed January 2, 2022.

11. https://www.gemini.com/cryptopedia/what-is-metaverse-crypto-nft-game-blockchain Accessed January 2, 2022.

12. https://www.textilegence.com/en/hm-opens-its-first-store-in-the-metaverse/ Accessed January 2, 2022.

13. https://www.theverge.com/22833369/nike-rtfkt-nft-sneaker-shoe-metaverse-company Accessed January 2, 2022.

14. https://www.theverge.com/2021/12/17/22843104/adidas-nfts-metaverse-sold-bored-ape Accessed January 2, 2022.

15. https://www.businesswire.com/news/home/20210909006012/en/Software-Products-Global-Market-Report-2021-COVID-19-Impact-and-Recovery-to-2030---ResearchAndMarkets.com Accessed January 9, 2022.

16. https://www.globenewswire.com/news-release/2021/03/31/2202641/0/en/Financial-Services-Global-Market-Report-2021-COVID-19-Impact-And-Recovery-To-2030.html Accessed January 15, 2022.

CHAPTER FOUR

EMBEDDED FINANCE IN THE OFFLINE WORLD

Embedded finance's suitability for online transactions and digital businesses was discussed in Chapter 3, but now we turn our attention to the world of brick-and-mortar businesses, which is probably the most exciting iteration of what embedded finance can offer. In 2019, Angela Strange, general partner at the venture capital firm Andreessen Horowitz, announced: "In the not-too-distant future, I believe nearly every company will derive a significant portion of its revenue from financial services."

Bain Capital Ventures' Matt Harris agrees. Strange didn't just mean Google and Apple. The ongoing Covid pandemic and the accompanying restrictions on activity placed severe stresses on offline businesses, but in the summer of 2021, with Covid still ongoing in most of the world, brick-and-mortar business still counted for 75% of retail transactions in the US. In Europe, the numbers are similar, with about two-thirds of retail transactions in 2021 taking place offline.[1]

A LOOK INTO THE FUTURE: THE SUPER APPS

It is no secret that China is well ahead of the West when it comes to having their life fully embedded into apps such as Alipay and WeChat. When asked what the day-to-day life of a person living in China powered by embedded finance looks like, Yassine Regragui, fintech specialist and expert on China, refers to his own experience:

> During my six years living in China, I never had to withdraw cash or use my bank card to pay, I only used Alipay or WeChat. I was a foreigner living in China, but could experience these two apps the same as a Chinese citizen. Ever since I connected my bank card to these apps, everything was possible. So what is possible with these apps? We can, of course, make in-store payments using QR codes. We can also make online payments. We can use insurance. We can have microloans. We can have investments, products, etc. But more than 50 percent of the time, we do not use the app for payments, instead we use it to book a cab, use public transports, talk with our doctors, communicate with our friends, rent an apartment, even formalize a marriage by signing such agreements within the app. So the possibilities are limitless. Also, all Chinese administrative services are provided on these apps. For example, the Chinese government relied on these two apps to initiate the COVID QR codes to

allow citizens to move freely when they didn't have some symptoms. On Alipay alone, there are more than 1000 features. Over one billion people in China are using those apps. So it means that there is a kind of value they get from it and that makes their life more convenient.

The question is: how does the rest of the world get to this level of embedded finance simplifying the lifestyle and life events of their citizens at the point of context, when they most need it?

THE DATA PLAY

Businesses with a digital presence are ideally suited to benefit from embedded finance because they have a great deal of customer data at their disposal. This data allows the business to predict future needs for the customer, to offer relevant deals and pricing for them based on those predictions, but also gives them the ability to offer a fairer and more tailored interest rate when it comes to providing them with a credit facility if they so chose to do so. Today, even offline merchants such as retailers include a digital component to their businesses and embedded finance can help them supercharge their customer's experience. Shoppers are asked for email addresses and phone numbers as ways to communicate rewards and boost loyalty. This will be discussed in more detail later, but for now we note that just as few businesses are truly "online-only" today, few businesses are also "brick-and-mortar-only."

Financial institutions can see a great deal into customers' lives, and receive strong indicators of life events. Still, in general, they have largely failed to predict customer needs and offer the right products at the right price at the right time due to outdated systems and processes. They can see which stores and brands merchants' customers spend the most money at frequently, how often they shop there, and how much they spend in each transaction, but crucially, they cannot see what specific products the customers are actually buying. The concept of what consumers are actually purchasing is often known as Level 3 data.

Let's discuss the three levels of data for a moment:

- Level 1 data is the merchant, or store, name and transaction amount.
- Level 2 data includes the merchant location, tax ID, and sales tax amount.
- Level 3 data includes the item description and quantity. Only merchants typically have access to Level 3 data.

This asymmetry of information is what puts so much potential power into the hands of merchants, especially those that customers trust and visit repeatedly. Merchants may not have anything like a complete view into customers' lives and spending habits, but in their specific area, they know a great deal.

If Sam goes to his local coffee shop every Monday through Friday and orders a double espresso and a croissant, the coffee shop can be proactive with Sam for future orders or know what to offer him as incentives for a certain amount of spend. It's a Saturday and Sam doesn't normally show up to the coffee shop. On Friday, the coffee shop could encourage Sam to show up on Saturday as well by offering him a free croissant with the purchase of his double espresso or on Sam's birthday (information the shop is likely to have if Sam provided the basic information when signing up as a frequent customer), the shop could do something special and custom for Sam, based on his spending habits throughout the year.

OFFLINE TO ONLINE

A few of the most striking trends regarding embedded finance in the offline world are:

- Cards
- Invisible Payments

- Checkout-Free In-Store Shopping
- Buy Now, Pay Later
- Internet of Things
- Insurance

In the pages that follow we will explore these trends more closely and look at relevant examples.

The Ancestor of Embedded Finance Offline: Cards

One of the first instances of embedded finance in a brick-and-mortar context came through payment cards issued by department stores. The "closed-loop cards," were also known as single-purpose cards because they could only be used in one location, at the department store. With closed-loop cards, merchants do not need a network such as Visa or Mastercard, nor do they need an issuing bank. The merchant acquiring bank is all that is needed, so terms for the merchant are very advantageous, resulting in better margins. The greatest benefit, however, is keeping the customer in the store's network and increasing their customer lifetime value or CLV. An in-store card can offer generous incentives or bonuses because of its advantageous terms. Have you ever been at a department store, maybe a Macy's or Best Buy, and upon checking out, been offered a store-branded card that offers you a significant percentage off the purchase you are about to make and an ongoing discount for all future purchases made at that shop? If it is a store that you frequent often, it might make sense because the discounts add up over time or if you are at a home improvement store like a Lowes or Home Depot and know you are going to make a large purchase to redo your kitchen, as an example, the offer is quite attractive.

Across the world, we still see closed-loop cards in play, though it has evolved somewhat. Starbucks is probably the most pre-eminent example.

The Starbucks card/wallet requires customers to load credit onto it, so it is prepaid, while most department stores are willing to offer credit. This way of doing business brings in tremendous revenue for Starbucks, and not just in lower-friction coffee and pastry sales. Starbucks holds about $1.5 billion in customer funds at any one time, and they held as much as $3 billion in December of 2020, as their cards are popular gifts for the holidays.[2] As with funds held by banks, this money can be claimed at any time, but meanwhile Starbucks is free to earn interest on it. These Starbucks accounts began as cards, but evolved into mobile wallets. While the world knows Starbucks as a coffee company with stores across the globe, in the years before Apple Pay, Starbucks was far and away the most successful mobile payments company in the world.

Invisible Payments

The most fundamental form of payment is the cash transaction, which still covers 20% of consumer spend in the US, even in a rapidly digitizing world.[3] In some countries, such as Japan and Germany, the number is far higher, while in Sweden and Singapore, it is rapidly approaching zero. Cash can typically not be used very easily in the digital economy, but it is possible, and with billions of cash-dependent customers around the world, it is still an essential form of payment. The problem with cash is that it yields the least data to merchants and none at all to issuers. Cash makes it difficult for merchants to form relationships with customers. For the greater privacy advocates, this is a feature, not a bug.

Invisible payments, also known as embedded payments, are the opposite of cash transactions. They are completed without the traditional handover of cash or even swipe of a payment card. They happen because of stored credentials: payment instruments, either cards or bank account information, that are stored with the merchant. They deliver a large amount of data to the merchant, who can use this to forge stronger bonds with customers.

Storing payment information with merchants, particularly involving bank accounts, involves trust, for obvious reasons. Payment information can be stored with an endless number of merchants, which is convenient, and carries many advantages, but not all merchants have the same protections and data security. The security has increased over time with the movement into the cloud with the likes of Amazon Web Services, Google Cloud, Microsoft Azure, and others, but recall the Target breach of 2013, in which the payment information of more than 40 million cardholders was compromised. This breach involved a flaw in the point-of-sale system provided to Target by a third party, and had nothing to do with storage of data for future use. In other words, storing data with merchants is not necessarily any more dangerous than making a single payment.

Many consumers were first introduced to invisible payments with the rise of Uber, which was founded in 2009 but rose rapidly in popularity in 2012. You may remember how game-changing it felt to use this service for the first time. Uber knew exactly how much to charge, told you this in advance, and the payment happened only when the ride was completed. There was no delay in finishing the ride, no taking time to find your card or cash, and no thinking about which payment method to use. Instead there was complete transparency in the amount you would be charged, right there on your mobile phone screen. To make this magical experience happen, the mobility company required users' payment card information to be preloaded into the app before use. This has now become common practice in many online services, but is less common in the offline world (but see Starbucks, above).

The appeal of invisible payments is undeniable: it's all about convenience. A buyer doesn't need to dig out her card or, in some cases, even mobile device—the payment simply happens.

If macroeconomic behavior teaches us anything, it is that convenience trumps most competing priorities (price and security are often but not always exceptions) and invisible payments offer today's busy shopper yet another advantage in the race to get through the day and get home faster. For this reason, data and trends show that invisible payments will continue to increase. The technology research firm Juniper Research estimated in Fall 2021 that invisible payments would process $78 billion transactions during the year, compared with about $10 billion in 2017. This represents growth of 700% in just four years.[4]

Matt Harris, Partner at Bain Capital Ventures, explains:

> Perhaps five years ago, the next leg of the journey became obvious. Once financial services were digital, they no longer needed to exist as discrete products; they could become embedded in software that consumers and businesses use all day long, and with which they have a durable and data-rich relationship. We are early in that process, and it requires imagination to see where it ends. For a while, it's just going to feel like everyone we do business with wants to offer us a debit card, make us a loan or help us save 15% on our car insurance.[5]

Eventually, though, when these products and services are all fully digital and embedded, the cognitive load of opening and managing these accounts will go away, as the operations are executed and automated by the software in which they are integrated.

In-Store Shopping: A Fully Checkout-Free Experience

The introduction of invisible payments in brick-and-mortar stores is a game changer. Invisible payments will continue to grow in importance because they offer advantages not just to consumers but to merchants as well. Invisible payments at the brick-and-mortar store means not just a faster checkout (which today, as in banking, often means self-service) but the possibility of no checkout at all.

Outside of offering a more convenient shopping experience for the customer, what does a checkout-free experience offer the store, i.e. the merchant? Checkout-free stores allow merchants to reduce personnel and free up space used for checkouts, providing more inventory for other items. Because items are tracked from the moment they are picked up, sellers can learn more about customer behavior and where to place items for optimum uptake. This concept of tracking items from the moment they are picked up is not new and one most of us are at least slightly familiar with. How many of us have gotten charges on our hotel bill from the minibar by grabbing that bottled water or box of peanuts for a late-night snack? Checkout-free stores take the minibar concept into the digital age. This additional customer data, tracking both inventory and customers, allows merchants to fine-tune their loyalty and rewards offerings on a highly granular level. Did customers pick up the name brand bag of chips to replace it with the generic brand later? The merchant could use the data to offer coupons or rewards on the name brand items in the future.

Due to the low number of checkout-free stores in existence today, only a small percentage of the population has shopped in one, but all evidence points to the expansion of these stores moving forward. What will your first checkout-free experience be like? Here's a sneak peak for the most curious of our readers.

In March 2021, with the Covid pandemic still in full force, Amazon opened cashierless Amazon Fresh stores in London. Featuring "Just Walk Out" technology, also known as Grab & Go, that allows shoppers to collect their goods and just walk out, Amazon Fresh stores caused something of a sensation, and not just in the UK, Media around the globe paid close attention. In a time when every additional human contact could be dangerous, or even fatal, shopping without the need to pause and scan goods or talk with a cashier seemed to respond to deeply held customer desires.

The idea is simple but the execution requires several interlocking systems of scanners. Upon entering the store, customers scan QR codes on their Amazon apps, which contain embedded payment information. A series of overhead cameras and sensors backed by artificial intelligence track users' progress through stores, tallying up purchases as they progress through the aisles. If a customer picks up an item, they must put it back in the same spot or they will be charged for the item. As an example, you can't pick up a banana and put it back in the apple section. When shoppers are done, they simply exit the store with their purchases, and the total value of the merchandise is charged to them via their apps. One shopper at an Amazon Fresh Store described the experience as positive and noted his receipt took about 20 minutes to appear after he left the store.

One of the things that makes Amazon Fresh so attractive for consumers is that it solves a primary problem that we are all acutely aware of—lines and dwell time. By allowing people to focus on the primary action or experience, in this case, picking up key grocery items, and having everything else be secondary (including the payment), you will have happier customers who will over a life cycle spend more money with fewer abandoned carts or frustration with scanning items themselves or other issues. The experience becomes more immersive and allows the retailer, Amazon Fresh or others, to focus on creating a more engaging experience while in store or offering a broader range of products.

Because they make checkout easier (or nonexistent) for customers, they reduce cart abandonment online and off, and encourage return visits. One 2018 estimate said removing checkout lines across the industry could bring in $37 billion in increased sales worldwide.[6] How many times have you been in a store with a cart full of items to get to the checkout line that is rows deep to decide that maybe tonight is takeout night? Customers waste hundreds of hours a year waiting in lines, and the Covid pandemic and digital shopping behaviors have reduced many shoppers' capacity for dealing with crowds and waiting long periods of time for items they can receive in other ways.

The idea of no checkout line at all is certainly an alluring one but what happens if someone tries to steal something? There must be a higher chance of theft with a checkout-free experience, right? It turns out that the opposite is true. Checkout-free stores are nearly impossible to steal from. Inventory is minutely tracked, and merchants can pinpoint when an item left the store and with whom, resulting in fewer losses to shrinkage and misplacement.[7] *Ars Technica* reporter, Sam Machkovech wrote an article about his experience with one of the checkoutless stores, Amazon Fresh, and his ability to trick the system by entering the bathroom and changing clothes.[8] The result was that Sam was only charged for the items he picked up prior to entering the bathroom, not what he picked up after changing. Of course there will be a minority that will find a way to game the system, but given the level and complexity of tracking in this new world era, the minority that beats the system will be less than the traditional checkout experience.

Author and commentator on digital financial services, Dave Birch believes this process needlessly violates customer privacy, because customers are identified rather than merely authenticated or credentialed. In other words, rather than saying, Ok, here is a shopper with a valid card who has permission to make a purchase, the store will say, "Oh, here's Dave Birch, maybe he'd like to buy some more pecans today." This is a tricky issue that may depend on customer comfort levels, and is a case of technology outrunning social etiquette.

At the time the Amazon Fresh cashierless experiment launched, experts in both the retail and payments worlds predicted Amazon would soon see competitors in the checkout-less market, either using technology purchased from Amazon, or a homegrown solution.[9] Time has proven these estimations correct. In the fall of 2021, Tesco, another major UK grocery chain, launched its GetGo stores, using very similar technology. The artificial intelligence in this case was said to build unique profiles of shoppers without using facial recognition software. Dave Birch would approve.

The insights gained from checkout-free stores mean that, to name just one example, tailored offers can be sent to users' apps based on the data in their profiles. And more stores are set to join, eliminating the pain point of the grocery checkout line. Around the time of the Tesco announcement, two other grocers, ALDI and Morrisons, also announced plans to go checkout-free.

While checkout-free stores are still in the experimental mode and far from ubiquitous, this is beyond the concept of innovation for the sake of innovation. Merchants employing checkout-free experiences learn more about their customers, offer them relevant deals, and ultimately sell more products.[10] With these successful early experiments, it is easy to see these experiences becoming the norm in the next few years. The future is bright for brick-and-mortar customers, and the merchants who serve them.

Buy Now, Pay Later

One of the most striking trends for both online and offline merchants that came to fruition in recent years is Buy Now, Pay Later, often shortened to BNPL. Merchants have struggled for years to get customers inside their own closed payment loop as described above, such as store cards, with few finding notable success. BNPL has enabled merchants to offer a similar function today. When BNPL emerged several years ago, first in Europe with the likes of Klarna and later in the US, many in the fintech space (and some still do) scoffed at the concept, calling it another name for layaway or installment plan purchasing, or just another form of consumer debt. While this may be true in the most basic sense of allowing consumers to purchase things they want today and pay for it over a period of time, the technology and methodology around BNPL have advanced quite drastically. There is no denying that entrepreneurs have built billion-dollar businesses on this model, and that it has found an enthusiastic customer base among credit-averse millennial and Gen Z shoppers. This group watched their parents and older siblings struggle with debt through the financial crisis of 2008–2009 that we have already seen was a major catalyst for the development of fintech.

Klarna

Founded: 2005
Valuation: $45.6 billion (October 2021)
Number of employees: 6,000

Early Approach

Klarna launched in Sweden with the mission to help consumers pay for online purchases with partial payments. Buyers set up installment payment plans with merchants and Klarna takes on the risk and interest if payments are missed. Klarna positions its products as more debit than credit, more like a utility bill that must be paid regularly rather than a large payment that continues to compound interest as portions are paid over time. Klarna's key customers include merchants the likes of H&M, Samsung, and Nike.

Klarna obtained a banking license in the EU in 2017. This move gives the company significant latitude to widen its product offerings among its existing customer base. Klarna has already expanded into the identity space, which positions it to serve as a payment wallet and checkout option across the internet. As of late 2021, Klarna is expected to become a public company in 2022.

One of the most important advantages of BNPL is a legacy of fintech innovation—transparency around pricing. We have already spoken of the banking industry's misalignment of incentives with its customer base. Banks are also notorious for hidden fees and fine print that no one in their right mind (other than lawyers and fintech nerds like us) reads.

Everything that can be said of banks is doubly true of credit cards, one of the banking industry's primary revenue drivers. Credit cards' ease of use and the ease of forgetting to pay off balances, have made credit cards the preferred payment form of millions of Americans and Europeans. In the US, for example, if you pay your balance every month, you benefit from rewards such as cashback and airline miles while paying no interest. But if, like millions of consumers—the vast majority of credit card users in the US—you carry a balance into the next month, you will be hit by high interest rates and quickly come to appreciate the downside of compound interest.

Buy Now, Pay Later looks to be an old offering by a new name, and it does have much in common with those earlier incarnations offered 50 or more years ago, but the payment landscape of retail sales has changed. Merchants are now forced to do business with the large payment networks who charge 2% or more for transactions. That means that for every payment you make for an item, 2% goes to the payment network behind the scenes. For businesses with narrow margins, that is a huge amount, which is why cash is preferred at so many businesses, especially mom and pop shops, even though managing cash carries costs and risks of its own. In major cities in the US, restaurants, nail salons, and corner shops prefer cash and incentivize you to pay that way by offering a lower price if you pay with cash. The expense of accepting cards also helps ensure the continued presence of checks at the point of sale in the US, which astounds visitors from other countries.

Fundamentally, BNPL results in customers spending more than they otherwise might, and to complete sales they might otherwise abandon. It widens consumer choices, and opens up products that might otherwise be out of reach. While some BNPL customers are wealthy, the majority are of limited means. A study from PYMNTS.com showed that 57% of BNPL customers earn less than $50,000 a year.[11]

BNPL offers merchants three crucial advantages over other forms of payment:

1. Merchants, unlike payment networks, have complete visibility into what customers are buying. This is the Level 3 data mentioned

above, also known as SKU-level data (SKU stands for stock-keeping unit). Getting access to this is the Holy Grail for loyalty and rewards, but Visa, Mastercard, and the banks do not have it. With this data, merchants can offer special deals on certain items to customers who want them. That level of specificity is rarely possible for others in the payment value chain.

2. BNPL forms its own payment network that operates in parallel to other payment rails. Customers can pay by directly linking to their bank, rather than a payment card (i.e. Visa or Mastercard). Alex Rampell of Andreessen Horowitz notes on Twitter that because of this, BNPL may be a gateway to a true payments revolution, and the most serious threat the payment networks have faced since cash. Currently BNPL operates simply, offering installment plans for repayment of borrowed funds. But BNPL payment systems have the potential to extend beyond point-of-service loans to other types of offerings unique to the businesses offering them. While we typically associate BNPL with large purchase items, the principle of the parallel payment rail directly to a bank account could be applied to even the smallest of transactions. As Rampell puts it, "Rather than a financing carrot, it might be a discount carrot, a warranty carrot, etc."[12]

3. BNPL also allows product manufacturers to have direct relationships with customers. While the internet similarly enabled direct relationships with customers, BNPL extends this to offline purchases as well. Take, for example, a bicycle manufacturer. With merchant cooperation, the manufacturer could learn of a brand enthusiast who has just purchased a new bicycle and extend special discounts, offers, or rewards for complementary products.

BNPL extends the relationship with customers beyond the point of purchase. A credit card customer may be paying off a major purchase years later, but she may have forgotten what the purchase was, and the merchant plays no part in that. BNPL means customers have a reason to come back to the store. Because loans are offered on singular products rather than baskets of goods, the customer retains a strong connection with the product, as opposed to paying off a portion of an amorphous credit card bill each month.

Merchants gladly front the money to customers for the purchase because it converts more customers and overcomes the reluctance of hesitant buyers. Merchants include this cost as part of their CAC or cost-of-acquisition and reallocate part of their marketing budget to cover the costs here. Consumers are happy with the relationship because, as previously discussed, there is a huge convenience for them being able to pay at the point of context. You walk into a store and see the TV you want. You are able to walk out of the store with that TV that day and the rest is background to the primary intention. You don't have to request a loan through a bank which may or may not be approved and in any case, can take a number of days or even weeks to hear back.

BNPL in Practice

What type of impact does BNPL have on merchants? Let's take a look at the high-end pet supplies manufacturer Whisker that charges $500+ for a self-cleaning litter box and unsurprisingly, its financing option has many takers. The company saw conversions increase 16% when it introduced BNPL financing through BNPL partner Affirm.[13]

Affirm

Founded: 2012
Market cap: $45.1 billion (October 2021)
Number of employees: 1,350

Early Approach

Affirm was a pioneer of Buy Now, Pay Later in the US and was founded by one of the original founders of PayPal, Max Levchin. Affirm has seen great success and went public in 2021. Launching initially at the point of sale, Affirm offered small installment loans with decisioning completed in seconds. Early clients of Affirm were the exercise equipment company famous for at-home bikes, Peloton, and the clothes retailer, Bonobos. Affirm evaluates nonstandard metrics for its underwriting, including social media posts and transaction data from payment accounts. Affirm assumes the risk for its merchants, and operates both in-store and online. In 2021, Affirm signed deals with both Target and American Airlines.

Affirm's value proposition to borrowers is low rates (typical rates in the space range from 2–8%) and transparency around fees. Merchants see larger purchasers, save on credit card fees, and form longer relationships with customers. Like many other fintech startups that began with a narrow focus, Affirm is widening its business. In 2021, Affirm began offering a debit card in partnership with Plaid and Marqeta. Affirm reports some, but not all of its loans to the credit bureaus.

Case Study: Katapult

Katapult is an example of another fintech operating in the BNPL space that offers bespoke BNPL products through a variety of retailers including the online houseware retailer Wayfair and computer makers Apple and Lenovo. The company began in the online space, but now operates both on and off, for example, in the brick-and-mortar Apple stores. Online was the initial focus for Orlando Zayas, CEO of Katapult, because Zayas felt this kind of shopper was rarely offered credit and if denied, had few alternatives. Katapult wanted to give all consumers credit, even those with historically poor records. When people are struggling financially and they need something, whether it is a repair to their car or other unexpected expense, paying directly is not always an option. Zayas positions Katapult as that source of funds, as an alternative to the payday lender.

Katapult's efforts at financial inclusion are courageous, but what truly sets Katapult apart is the customization it allows customers. Zayas shares why the standard formula for BNPL doesn't work for his customers:

> Most of the way I categorize BNPL is that it's "Split it into four payments over eight weeks," using your debit card or your credit card. That solves a certain issue if you want to buy a hundred-dollar pair of jeans to go out this weekend. You could split the payments over eight weeks. It's simple, it's easy to understand, but it doesn't work very well when you're trying to buy more high-dollar goods like appliances and furniture. It's hard for especially the non-prime consumer to split a thousand-dollar refrigerator over eight weeks, and four payments, that's almost impossible. So we think that from a BNPL perspective, there's tranches, if you will, of satisfying consumer demand. That's the $300 and less transactions, and then the over-$300 transactions. Where we come in is handling those over-$300 transactions for this non-prime consumer.

BNPL firms take a lot of criticism for just offering another way for consumers to get into debt, but Zayas's mission for the company is to truly be of service to customers.

Zayas says:

> One of the things that we're focused on in the next few years is the customer journey on improving their credit or just becoming

more financially independent and less reliant on financing or other things. We believe in giving the tools to the customer to get the things that they need, but then also helping them along that journey to look at other products, educate them on credit cards, savings accounts and checking accounts, and getting the best deal for their money. Many of these customers are either young or they had a situation that happened and they fell into it, and we want to help them get out of that and get back up into saving money.

Education is a key concern for Zayas, who wants to keep his customers close in order to expose them to the kind of financial education that will someday make Katapult's BNPL product unnecessary.

According to Zayas:

One of the things that we don't talk about a lot to our customers now, but we will, is just general financial aptitude. Things like the importance of investing in your 401K. If your company matches, that's the best thing you can do from an investment perspective. And then just savings and building your credit and focusing on your credit, because credit is so important, and I don't think it's going away anytime soon.

Ultimately, Zayas says he wants Katapult's legacy to be that it helps its customers build a better life.

As with everything else fintech-related, this industry is cyclical, and banks are taking a piece of the BNPL pie. While banks like JP Morgan Chase, the largest retail bank in the US, joined the BNPL movement, the challenge still remains on the exact use case. Banks typically do not know what a customer has purchased (though they can often make good guesses). Banks may miss some benefits of BNPL, but cutting down on cart abandonment and increasing spend per card may still make the endeavor worthwhile. Chase, with its massive card portfolio, is willing to take the chance.

In the online world, PayPal, which is in a very similar position to banks in terms of limited visibility into customer carts, has been offering BNPL for many years without great fanfare. PayPal has had a front row seat to cart abandonment for several decades now. Increased customer spend and reduced abandonment clearly bring in enough revenue to make extending credit worthwhile. There is an argument to be made that banks that say no to BNPL as they have said no to personal loans will miss out on BNPL's considerable advantages to financial institutions.

You may be wondering, what happens if consumers can't make their payment for that new couch they bought? You aren't alone and it certainly happens. Critics of the BNPL movement often focus on the high percentage of people who are delinquent on their payments. Customers who miss payments on BNPL loans enter the same collections process used by other types of lenders. Credit Karma noted in a 2021 report that 44% of its customers had used a BNPL service, and 34% of those borrowers had missed at least one payment.[14] Affirm noted in the same period that non-delinquent loans, meaning loans with no missed payments, made up 95% of its book. But all lenders know the losses from one bad loan can erase the revenue from many good loans. Now, let's take a look at another company in the space, Katapult.

The Internet of Things

The Internet of Things is the network of connected devices in the world around us. These are everyday objects, not computers or mobile phones. They may be stationary or moving, useful in their own right, or only as a point of internet connection. We will walk through examples of each of these kinds of products. While right now there are a handful of examples that really showcase embedded finance in practice, soon, there will be many more, and they will be so ubiquitous in our lives that we may not even be aware of them.

Our world is full of internet-connected devices that act as a field of sensors detecting the activities of individuals going about their day. In a way it is a marketer's dream, since data is the name of the game for sales and marketing today. What do you know about your prospect? Can you anticipate her wants? Can you prove yourself valuable enough so that she seeks you out?

To some, this activity is by its very nature nefarious because it impinges on privacy (but what is privacy when your mobile phone manufacturer, service provider, and various apps know exactly where you are and even how many steps you took that day?). While privacy concerns are valid, tracking customers is not necessarily sinister. It is an activity of commerce and an opportunity to meet customer needs more efficiently than ever before. As author and commentator on digital financial services Dave Birch noted earlier, sometimes we are asked for more information than is necessary (and sometimes we volunteer more).

Companies in certain industries enjoy privileged insights into the day-to-day movements of people. The transportation space, particularly the automotive space, is an innovation hotspot for the simple reason that we as consumers spend a lot of time moving, whether driving or taking public transportation. On public transit systems across the globe, commuters can use stored payment credentials to access subways, buses, and trams, or to pay for parking. Where once coins had to be dug out of pockets and purses and forced into grimy germ-laden slots, now mobile phones or cards waved near sensors suffice. This doesn't mean the transactions are faster—indeed, it's often the opposite—but it does mean travelers don't need to remember to carry a fistful of coins or bills, standing in long lines to get a metro card and leave with leftover balance, and can avoid touching devices shared by many others throughout the course of a day.

Take the case of driving. The Department of Transportation estimated in 2017 that Americans spent an average of 1.1 hours a day driving, which cumulatively works out to more than 17 days a year behind the wheel.[15] (Americans drive about twice as many miles per year compared to Germans, who cover the most distance on the road in Europe.) With 5,000 miles of toll roads in the US, a frequent pain point for drivers is sitting in traffic waiting to toss coins into a plastic receptacle or hand them to a toll collector.

Electronic toll collection (ETC) devices, such as EZPass, used in the Eastern United States, California's FasTrack, France's Liber-t, and Spain and Portugal's VIA-T to name just a few, save their users both time and money. An inexpensive plastic device that is loaded with an individual's payment credentials is placed on the windshield of your vehicle. Every time the vehicle passes a certain point, usually but not always a toll charging a specific sum, payment is deducted from the connected account. The amount charged by ETCs is often discounted from the cash payment rate. This may seem surprising, since cash earns discounts for purchases such as gasoline, but electronic payments have greatly reduced the cost and risk to toll collection companies of storing and transporting physical currency, not to mention staffing toll booths.

Without EZPass, FasTrack, Liber-t, or VIA-T, drivers need to wait in line to hand over cash to an agent. This is a convenience users are willing to pay for, and they do, depositing lump sums of money into EZPass accounts to be used when needed, similar to the cards and apps used by Starbucks and other quick-service coffee restaurants. Customers are willing to load hundreds of dollars at a time because they use the product on a consistent basis or they acquire a pass at a rental car agency to ease the friction of travel even if only for a few days. The Pennsylvania Turnpike Authority said in 2020 that 86% of drivers on its roads used EZPass.[16] Many exits on the Pennsylvania Turnpike are only available to EZPass customers, meaning cash customers will need to drive out of their way simply because they are cash users. FasTrack in California is particularly aggressive in removing any alternative payment option—you either use FasTrack or a photo is taken of your license plate and you are sent an invoice for more money (payable by check or card). Some of the

European systems are using direct debit to the user-linked account to pay for the toll fee and in the near future it is probable that open banking, in which third parties can access consumers' funding accounts, will be used to trigger a payment initiation from the user account every time she crosses a Liber-t or VIA-T point of control.

EZPass is also used to measure and optimize traffic flow, as are mobile phones and internet-connected cars. Conduent, the company that operates EZPass, can share this data with municipalities in order to determine where motorists are getting slowed down or stuck. So-called smart cities can use all the data generated by moving residents to eliminate bottlenecks and optimize the flow of people, goods, and services. Some municipalities, of which Singapore is a notable example, have taken this concept quite far and serves as an example for others to follow.

Transit data in cities is enriched by information provided by stored credential payments. Where previously a transit system might know how many people entered the system at Station A and exited at Station B, now it can know who entered at Station A and exited at Station B. Smart cities can utilize data from bike rentals, such as London's Santander Bike and New York City's Citibike, transit systems such as London's TFL (which was also one of the first in the world to implement contactless payment from one's payment card), and toll collection points, to gauge where people need to get to, and when. While this data may not be of much use to New York City, cities such as Singapore and Berlin, with some of the best transit systems in the world, have embraced the use of data in smart city strategies to improve travel for residents and visitors.

The network of data receptors that is the Internet of Things is a precursor to a future where everything is connected and at the consumer's fingertips. Invisible payments have the ability to make life smoother and more efficient. It is notable that payments are rarely shown in science fiction movies and TV shows, because they are, naturally, embedded and invisible.

The Connected Car: Tesla and Beyond

Connected vehicles such as those in Tesla's electric fleet offer numerous opportunities for IoT and embedded finance. Like any device with stored payment credentials, internet-connected cars can make purchases with the driver-user's consent, often using spoken commands.

While some users may doubt the utility of a smart oven or smart refrigerator, few debate that connected vehicles can improve their driving experience. Tesla's vehicles not only warn drivers of traffic jams and optimal routes, but also report on weather hazards such as tornadoes and hurricanes.

Tesla

Founded: 2003
Market cap: $1.05 trillion (Jan. 2022)
Number of employees: 70,750

Early Approach

The market capitalization of Tesla, founded in 2003, recently surpassed that of General Motors (founded 1908) by 10x. While some of Tesla's recent meteoric rise in value may be attributed to its high-flying CEO Elon Musk and the company's ongoing flirtation with cryptocurrency, which is skyrocketing in value in late 2021 amid inflation fears, some of it can be attributed to Tesla's unsurpassed "hyper-connectivity." Tesla cars, even more than competing contemporary vehicles, are highly sophisticated pieces of technology. Tesla, unlike most of its competitors, is valued by investors and the market like a technology company, not like an automaker.

Automobiles have incorporated increasing amounts of computer hardware and software every year for the last decade, but Tesla leapfrogged them all by embracing cryptocurrency, open-source software, cloud computing, and self-driving, powered by machine learning. As with a mobile phone, Tesla software is updated frequently, and remotely. This tech-forward approach positions it ahead of other manufacturers, and Wall Street clearly approves.

Musk's ambitions are huge, and we can expect Tesla to continue experimenting with bleeding-edge technology. Its smart vehicles will connect with IoT access points in smart cities, and its machine learning will assist in ordering everything from charges to parts for repair to food to anniversary gifts. The connected car will also be connected to the connected home. Tesla is as much a battery company, or energy company, as it is a car manufacturer, and Tesla will increasingly play a role in smart homes. It already offers the wall battery, which serves as a generator when the home loses power. With drivers spending more time in traffic, the always-connected Tesla with embedded payment information will play an ever-larger role in commerce.

Connecting Cars and Payments

We are seeing more and more how IoT is playing a role in embedded finance, but there is another way that traditional industries can have a piece of the pie. Other car manufacturers are getting involved from a different lens, starting with payments. As we know, a car is typically the second largest purchase we have as individuals in our lifetime and car manufacturer Volvo has taken the opportunity to turn that model on its head.

Volvo offers an alternative to buying or leasing a car and instead has a subscription car service called "Care By Volvo." There is no down payment or long-term contracts. Through the subscription service, everything related to your car experience is included—things like auto insurance, maintenance, protection for the tires, wheels, breakdown issues—all are included if you subscribe to the car. Michael Jackson, the former COO of Skype and non-executive director on the board for Volvo sees a strong comparison to the world of communications as he says:

> 20 years ago, if you wanted to make a phone call, you had to go to the phone on your desk and pick it up and use the phone company AT&T. Now phone calls and communications are built into everything we know. This is true wherever you are, there is a chat function built into websites, there is a click to chat button within your car. You are not using the phone company any longer. This is what embedded finance is all about.

What does that mean for the Volvo driver with a subscription? Michael says: "It means they pay their fee to get their car and it automatically comes out of their bank account. But it also means that whenever extra services are used, whenever you do, it gets automatically managed. Parking is automatically debited, extra software in the car is automatically debited, functionalities debited, etc." Why does this work? Because the customer doesn't care to be involved in these details and frankly, there is no reason they need to be.

As to the importance of embedded finance for car manufacturers and beyond, Michael says, "Embedded finance is definitely what we're going to see in 20 years time, the same way as we have seen with embedded communication. You need to build payments and other core financial service components naturally into your product. You just need to. It's what people expect."

Let's move over to an iconic brand in the automobile space, McLaren. Why would McLaren want to get into financial services? For starters, racing is quite an exclusive sport. Stadiums only hold a limited capacity, and merchandising is quite limited to things like hats, shirts, etc. While McLaren has great success with Formula One and racing, they are much more than that. They are also a world class engineering company for new materials, manufacturing techniques, etc. How could a brand like McLaren expand their fanbase? McLaren and others like them are finding other ways to engage and expand fan bases outside of the traditional path through channels like eSports. There are virtual races happening 24 hours a day. Why not offer McLaren skins and reward the McLaren skinned car when they win? That reward could then be converted into local currency and spent by the person collecting the rewards.

As Nigel Verdon, CEO of Railsbank, the primary partner and enabler for McLaren to get into financial services, puts it: "It's about developing the relationship between McLaren and the fans. It is not just engagement. It's about revenue. It's about repeat purchases. You learn about the consumer, learn about their wallet and their spending habits. It's about giving the consumer the experience and then using the experience to benefit the consumer and the business."

This model has real revenue potential. Let's say that McLaren has 1 million fans and through embedded finance and this multichannel approach, McLaren can make $1/mo from each fan. That is $12 million dollars a year. Now imagine this at an even greater scale. Let's take the most popular football/soccer team in the world, Manchester United. According to research from the global market research agency, Kantar, Manchester United has a global fanbase of 1.1 billion as of 2019, some estimate that number to be 1.5 billion now.[17] For simplicity's sake, let's use the 1 billion number. Imagine tapping into this fanbase through embedded finance and making even 25 cents a month? That's revenue of $250 million a year.

Embedded finance is also a consumer data play. Sticking with the McLaren example, if you have data on your fans and can see what they are doing, where they are spending money on their cards and on what they are spending on, you can use that data to offer them incentives that are directly relevant to them in a meaningful way. Moreover, if the fan is back at the same racing track physically or virtually in the eSports stadium, you as a brand have a clearer idea on where to place merchandise or advertising. Best yet, the data just discussed becomes owned by the brand as opposed to third parties.

The Internet of Things at Home

The Internet of Things is also sprouting up around the home, typically, at first, in luxury items such as the Samsung refrigerator and stove. Alexa, the virtual assistant technology distributed by Amazon, which takes the form of a speakerphone at home, has allowed its users to pay for things they were ordering on Amazon vocally for a long time. Alexa is indeed linked to payment details stored on Amazon, enabling a smooth payment experience to order whatever a user wants on Amazon itself. Users can now employ the Alexa app to pay their bills by just asking their speakerphone or mobile device.[18] But as with robotics, internet-connected devices can also be made very cheaply and very small. In 2015, Amazon took an early stab at providing fingertip convenience in the home via embedded payment credentials with its Dash buttons. These were simple plastic buttons that cost $5 each and contained adhesives to stick on refrigerators, washing machines, or anywhere else. Users could re-order detergent or toilet paper with the click of a button, a dream for the homeowners of previous generations. The information was stored in the user's Amazon account, to make re-ordering as simple as possible. Why is this example of effortless convenience no longer with us? One issue was that many Dash-using parents found their children were fond of clicking the buttons. Repeatedly. Endless supply of dish detergent, anyone?

While it may not seem like a significant problem for the industry at large, the role of children ordering goods and services using stored payment credentials is indeed one of the stumbling blocks of invisible payments, and has even made its way into popular culture. The 2017 film, *Diary of a Wimpy Kid: Long Haul*, features two children using their parents' phone to summon an Uber and take a long and expensive journey, while telling each other, "It's free!"

Dash buttons were widely ridiculed soon after their release, and called dystopian, and were ultimately discontinued. The *New Yorker* quipped, "The idea of shopping buttons placed just within our reach conjures an uneasy image of our homes as giant Skinner boxes, and of us as rats pressing pleasure levers until we pass out from exhaustion."[19] But more pointedly, a Danish court found that Dash buttons violated consumer protection laws because the action of clicking to order provided no information about costs, which might have changed since the previous order, or include hidden or unexpected fees. Virtual assistants such as Alexa offer greater utility and can serve a similar function—but, unless asked, they offer no more information about the cost of products than Dash buttons.

Dash buttons and the virtual assistant devices prefigure smart homes equipped with arrays of sensors and internet connections to merchants that frictionlessly deliver goods via embedded payments. Coffee makers and washing machines will re-order supplies on their own. It is simple to add on services to existing orders, as with warranties, insurance, or more complex financial products. The home will be the venue for these transactions, as the home has become the venue for so much economic activity in recent years.

Insurance

Much like financial services, insurance at the point of context, whether when driving or renting a car or booking a trip, is extremely relevant for consumers and customers. When a purchase is made and the customer is thinking about the product and the company, the right insurance can be offered and chances of uptake are much higher in that moment in real time as opposed to a paper notice arriving weeks later, out of mind, out of context.

Of McKinsey's estimated $7 trillion market opportunity for embedded finance by 2030, insurance accounts for over 40% of that, at $3 trillion.[20] Why? The reason for this lies primarily in that insurance enjoys a huge greenfield. Many younger and underbanked people are underinsured, and technology and data now mean underwriting and the products associated with them can be more efficient and tailored to specific needs. Imagine buying a TV from a brand you love that you have multiple touchpoints with, and the next time you engage, you are offered an insurance product (Figure 4.1). When the service is tied to a product and company you love, you are much more likely to click Yes.

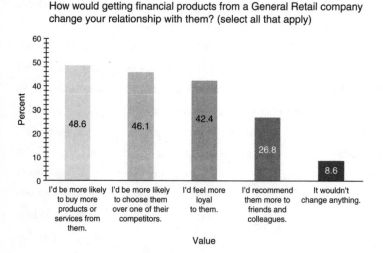

Figure 4.1 Most consumers would think more positively of a retailer that provided them with financial services.

Source: Cornerstone Advisors.

How does embedded insurance play out in the future and who will it impact? Florian Graillot, founding partner at Astorya.vc, notes that even with the advantages of embedded insurance, not every customer will be targeted and benefit. He says:

> I believe it's very important to keep that in mind that we are not saying that all the industry will switch online. We are just seeing that customers are in need of digitization at one point. In terms of what penetration to target, it is probably best to look at retailers and e-commerce. As of 2021, let's say 30–50% of the total retail market is now done through e-commerce. These are the type of numbers we can target for insurance and we could even start with a more modest 10–20%.

While this is a rather small percentage, the opportunity is still huge with the insurance market in Europe. As Jennifer Rudden shares in her Statista article: "The gross written premiums of the European life-insurance companies in 2018 amounted to 764 billion euros. In the non-life segment of the market, premiums amounted to approximately 407 billion euros, which constituted just over half of the life premiums value. During 2018, almost 704 billion euros was paid out in life insurance benefits in Europe."[21] We are seeing numbers like this across the globe and the opportunities in this space are vast.

There is the ability to get quite specific and granular with the opportunities within embedded insurance offering specific products for specific use cases. This is particularly true for companies across industries who own the market or have large market share. What areas or products could take off first? It is a safe guess to bet on pocket products, devices or things you always have with you—your watch, your phone, etc. When purchasing devices like this, you are often asked if you want to pay for insurance to cover any damage or excessive wear and tear. This covers many physical goods beyond phones and moves into areas like bicycles. If you purchase a $500 bike, it is normal to be asked if you would like to add insurance on your bike for incidental damages. More and more, customers are accustomed to being asked for such things as part of the checkout process. As Florian puts it, "If you are selling bikes, you are very relevant to sell bike insurance. If you are selling home improvement, you are relevant to sell home insurance. If you are Fitbit or any health wearable, you are relevant to sell either life or health insurance policies."

Embedded Insurance in Practice

We are seeing an abundance of insurtech startups across the continent of Europe from the UK, to Germany, to France and beyond. Bought by Many, an insurtech startup based in the UK, has already accumulated hundreds of thousands of customers. Get Safe, an insurtech startup in Germany offering insurance products focused on bicycle, home, and electronics, has more than 250,000 customers in Germany alone. In France, insurtech Luko, focused on home insurance, has more than 200,000 customers. While these are still small figures compared to the incumbent insurance providers like AXA or Alliant who have millions of customers, the collective power of these new entrants shows that there is certainly a demand to buy directly from these insurtech startups.

Qover

Founded: 2016
Valuation: $118 million
Number of employees: 87

Early Approach

Qover states on its LinkedIn page that "we build our own embedded insurance products using open APIs to help fast-growing digital companies – hacking insurance to make it simpler, smarter and more accessible."

Qover has grown quite aggressively over the last year and has raised over €35 million and now offers solutions across 32 European countries. Qover counts Revolut and Deliveroo among its clients, and is active in the gig economy and the soft mobility space, a category that includes rentals, scooters, and bikes, and is a strong vertical in European cities.

Insurtech startups like Qover, established in 2016 out of Belgium, is a great example of the traction we are seeing with embedded insurance. One of the more exciting partnerships Qover has entered into is with Revolut, the biggest neobank in Europe valued at over $5.5 billion, as of early 2022. As with other products that Revolut and other neobanks offer, there is a seamless customer experience that is easy to access and understand. Companies with large customer bases like Revolut, that has more than 15 million customers, want to embed insurance because they see it as an additional product allowing them to generate margin on their existing customer base. In the case study on the Qover website, the Qover team further outlines why Revolut chose them.[22] As they state: "Revolut wanted a partner who was capable of offering innovative insurance solutions across 32 European countries through a single technical integration – an impossible mission for a traditional insurance company." As Florian Graillot, founding partner at Asorya.vc puts it, "If you are a platform or company with an existing customer base and need to generate additional revenues on your existing base, insurance is a very accurate way to do this. Contrary to the banking space, insurance is the margin product."

What does the Revolut insurance product look like in detail? According to the use case, "the insurance solution is fully integrated into the banking app allowing users to access the 3 new insurance products in real-time from 'Plus', 'Premium' and 'Metal' accounts." Revolut customers are able to view details about their insurance policy including all legal documents, in one easy-to-find place. To add to the all-in-one mentality, "the Qover team has put in place technology enabling Revolut customers to report, track and control claims directly in the app. A push notification system allows users to be informed at every stage of the claims process." This is a prime example of going back to the basic principle of meeting the customer where they are in a way that is convenient to them and enhances their experience.

The US has several new insurance companies that offer quick decisioning as well as mobile and embedded experiences. New York–based Lemonade raised nearly half a billion dollars before going public in the summer of 2020. In its S-1 filing the company writes, "By leveraging technology, data, artificial intelligence, contemporary design, and behavioral economics, we believe we are making insurance more delightful, more affordable, more precise, and more socially impactful. To that end, we have built a vertically-integrated company with wholly-owned insurance carriers in the United States and Europe, and the full technology stack to power them." Lemonade offers full functionality through the Lemonade API and is embedded in the sites of rental and moving companies. Lemonade also offers home and auto insurance, all done with a few clicks on its mobile app, or embedded in another's app. While its stock had a difficult 2021 as Wall Street fretted about an overheated housing market, Lemonade's market cap is still $2.2 billion, as of early 2022.

Ornikar

Founded: 2013
Valuation: $750 million
Number of employees: 229

Early Approach
Per its LinkedIn page, Ornikar "transforms the driving experience to become the essential partner of automotive mobility: we support you throughout your learning to drive and up to the insurance

of your vehicle, and reinvent this experience in France, Spain and soon all over the world!"

Ornikar began as a driving school and an inexpensive way to get your driver's license, then used that data and experience to move into auto insurance. Currently the insurance is only available in France, but as the schools are all over Europe, insurance should soon follow.

There are great examples of embedded insurance already at place from nontraditional brands as well. Ornikar started out as a driving school for young drivers and the company had so much traction they started selling car insurance for their young drivers. This also proved to be successful to the point the company raised a hundred million–plus euros and is now an insurance distributor themselves offering insurance products to all drivers.

Why was Ornikar successful in getting into embedded insurance? They followed the principle of addressing the market need first and then built insurance on top of it. A suggested approach for any companies that have a desire to get into insurance is to follow the guiding principles: Start with addressing the market need, then solving for the customer problem, then focus on building the right technology and product to address that need and the last step is then to plug in the insurance capacity to it.

Ping An

Founded: 1988
Market cap: $149 billion
Employees: 360,000

Early Approach

Ping An is a technology company that first started selling insurance, pioneering the sale of Western-style insurance in China. They made the move to enabling any platform starting with their own ecosystem and had the biggest marketplace for selling second-hand cars and the biggest platform for reconciliation.

Ping An offers embedded finance in reverse. It began with insurance then branched out into non-financial services, and now offer a wide suite of products for consumers and businesses, including health and health insurance.

Case Study: Ping An

Ping An in China got its start in insurance before branching out to adjacent industries such as healthcare. The company's chief innovation officer, Jonathan Larsen, described the state of insurance in China, and how it can be a starting point to offer more financial services. "We think the next phase of insurance in China is going to be increasingly creating real-world services, as many as possible that can actually be digitally delivered, that instantiate the financial offerings that we have and come as part of them."

Larsen also described a program developed for its automobile insurance clients. "Another example might be in auto insurance, where we've got this Good Driver application," Larsen said.

> We have about 50 million people who are enrolled in this platform. About half of them are customers. The rest are prospects. It's a pretty rich platform that allows you to access a lot of auto-related services, among which are our telematics platform, which basically allows us to use an opt-in kind of mobile app to monitor drivers' performance and behavior and assess their risk. And we're able to use that to create incentives

for people to become lower-risk drivers. We're also able to use it to drive positive selection.

China is no less competitive in its hunt for profitable customers than Europe or the US. Ping An's existing services give it a leg-up in locating those prospects. It's nearly always easier and cheaper to cross-sell existing customers than to onboard new ones. "We're able to use this platform as a way of engaging clients and bringing them closer to us and building a non-financial relationship, which is, you know, one step closer to building a financial relationship," Larsen said. "So that might be another example where we've been able to take non-financial services and connect them to financial offerings."

Ping An has also moved from insurance to the health industry. Healthcare is one of the world's hottest businesses. Even though many countries offer free or massively subsidized healthcare, there will always be certain paid procedures and certain customers, usually extremely wealthy ones, who purchase services outside of the system. "One of the reasons we got into health was as an extension of our own health insurance business in China, which is where our company is overwhelmingly based—private health insurance," Larsen said. He continued:

> It's still a pretty decent category. It's still less than 10 percent of the total health value of the country, the government being 50 percent and the balance being out of pocket. And what we were looking for was a way of reaching a much broader target market or addressable market than the current private health insurance market would allow us to do. And we were successful in building the thing on the Good Doctor platform, which now has more than 400 million registered users and is the largest such platform in the world.

What is intriguing about Ping An is that, in a way, it is operating embedded finance in reverse, using a financial services platform in insurance to sell non-financial services products. Larsen states:

> Now that we have that platform, we're able to offer that as a feature and service offering embedded within our health insurance offerings, as well as some of our life and PNC (or Primary and Noncontributory) offerings that have health dimensions to them. So I think that's an example of where, on the one hand, the genesis of the Good Doctor came out of kind of a strategic impetus around thinking about how actual services and financial services could co-exist and interact. We're now at a point where we've got our first scale platform in primary care consultation, the first level of consultation, and we think it's a pretty valuable add-on to the financial offerings that we have.

THE IMPACT OUTSIDE FINANCIAL SERVICES

As the examples above showcase, from traditional retail brick-and-mortar businesses to insurance companies, the opportunities to embed finance into everyday life is enormous. Below are examples of other traditional industries where embedded finance can have an impact: healthcare, media, and telecom.

Healthcare

Healthcare is a sector that has a huge opportunity to move from antiquated ways into the digital world and embedded finance can help it to do so. One such company that exemplifies this is Peachy Pay.

Case Study: Peachy Pay

Lex Oiler, founder and CEO of Peachy Pay, knows well how antiquated the healthcare system is. She says:

> In 2017, I had a $144 medical bill go to collections—not because I didn't have the funds to pay it, but simply because I didn't see the bill. Amidst the craziness of having a baby, a bill slipped through the cracks somehow. I don't know if it was lost in the mail, sent to the wrong address, or simply never sent at all. I only know that I was left with a ding on my credit report for years. When I finally learned about the bill, I ended up calling nine different collection agencies with a credit card in hand, trying to find somebody that would let me pay the bill. At the end of it all, because nobody could figure out who owned the debt, a collection agent simply deleted the tradeline from my credit report.

Lex's story is a prime example of what we talk about when we discuss the importance of being customer-first and offering an experience that is seamless and transparent. The healthcare billing world generally does not offer these experiences, and that's unfortunate. The industry in the US is massive. While Lex's example is one from the medical space, these bills, and the collection calls that follow when they are unpaid, can come from many places: an overdue cable bill, car loan, etc.

Lex continues:

> I thought there must be some regulatory reason that kept healthcare from moving on from this antiquated process, but as I began researching the problem, I realized that this wasn't the case. Instead, I discovered that healthcare is just really slow and incredibly resistant to change. To me, the solution was reasonably clear. Nearly every adult in the United States has a smartphone in their pocket. We're all used to shopping online from our phones; why not apply a similar experience to healthcare? As

I dug deeper into the provider side of the problem, it became clear that this wasn't just a patient problem, but that providers were struggling too! With the prevalence of high deductible plans rising steadily over the past decade, providers were being asked to collect more and more of their fees directly from their patients. And they were leaving a significant amount of money on the table by sticking with the status quo.

In this case, embedded finance can add a tremendous amount of value on both sides of the marketplace, not just for the end consumer but also for the provider, including the doctor's offices. Technology that can help people pay their bills more easily while also making it easier for patients and providers to connect around bill payment so that providers can send and manage the bills makes a lot of sense.

But the payments piece is just step one for Peachy. Lex says, "From the beginning of building Peachy, providers have been asking about lending options. It's clear that patients need alternative ways to pay for healthcare." This is not surprising. According to a 2021 *New York Times* article, "collection agencies held $140 billion in unpaid medical bills last year."[23] The article goes on to say that "between 2009 and 2020, unpaid medical bills became the largest source of debt that Americans owe collections agencies." They are also the largest source of bankruptcy.

Currently the process is almost entirely manual. Patient financing typically comes in two forms: in-house payment plans offered by the provider, or loans from healthcare lenders. In both cases, the process can be quite painful for providers. As Lex shares:

Suppose a provider wants to provide patients with a payment plan. In that case, they usually do so on an ad hoc basis, simply agreeing to terms on a one-off basis and tracking the terms internally somewhere, often in a spreadsheet or calendar.

Then the provider's staff has to remember to charge the patient's card according to the agreed-upon schedule. It's a nightmare for providers.

For the providers that don't want to deal with this headache and instead choose to offer third-party products for loans, it is possible, but the process is still quite manual and is certainly not a seamless experience. Providers will direct patients to the third party's website and ask them to submit an application either on site in the office (much like we have seen at the point of sale, or POS, in a retail environment) or the application will be sent home with the patient to do on their own, which of course dramatically lowers the likelihood of adoption and now the patient is at home alone trying to figure out how to apply for a loan—not necessarily an ideal customer experience.

This whole experience introduces a significant amount of friction into the payment process. Patients have to ask for flexible options, instead of having them as default offerings. This can present a level of shame or embarrassment for patients in difficult financial circumstances. And on the provider end, the process of implementing and offering such options is a headache. Lex continues: "Patients and providers both just want an easy way to pay for healthcare, so offering financing options within the digital payment process reduces the friction for patients and providers. Patients then have easy access to financing without jumping through any additional hoops, and providers no longer have to administer the offered financing options manually."

So how does Peachy, that focuses on the payments piece, plan to address this opportunity? Through partnership, of course. In this case, with another fintech player, Walnut that refers to themselves as "Healthcare Now: Pay Later," according to their website.[24] As Lex shares:

> Peachy's partnership with Walnut allows us to offer patients ethical financing options within our current payment flow. By integrating Walnut into our product, we can provide patients with basically any payment scenario they could dream of, without ever leaving Peachy's payment flow. Instead of asking patients to leave the payment process to find financing, we simply integrate the financing options into the existing bill pay function. You can easily apply for financing, receive an instant approval or denial, select your terms, and make your first payment, all from within the safety of the Peachy interface.

The flow just described is a prime example of embedded finance at work at the point of convenience for the end customer, in this case, the patient.

But what does this look like for the provider? Lex continues:

> When providers offer Patient Financing Powered By Walnut, patients have the option to (1) pay the bill in full via debit card, credit card, Apple Pay, or Google Pay, (2) set up a payment plan of 3-, 6-, 9-, or 12-month terms, and now (3) apply for financing options of up to 36 months. Patients shouldn't have to leave the Peachy portal while paying for healthcare. We want to give them everything they need to make informed decisions about paying for their healthcare.

With the market cap of healthcare bills continuing to skyrocket, this market is prime for embedded finance to be more seamlessly integrated into the process, and we are just at the beginning. With more and more integration (think health data and others), the future is bright and the opportunities endless, all with the goal of having a better customer experience, and reducing financial hardship and bankruptcies.

Media

Few industries were as profoundly upended by the internet as the music industry. When music went digital with the likes of Spotify, Apple Music, etc., the role of the record label changed profoundly, but they are still critical for the industry. Just because a business model shifts, it doesn't mean that core components are no longer valuable, they just change shape. Media and music are another great example of an industry ripe with opportunity for embedded finance. In the age of streaming, music creators see far less direct revenue from fans in terms of album or song purchases and fees from live performances, and the time it takes artists to get paid for their work is often long. Instead, the funds go to platforms such as Spotify, which sets the pay scales for creators. As dominant platforms grow in strength, content creators face similar challenges across all creative fields. This has led to the rise of platforms like Patreon, in which consumers of media can directly pay the creators themselves, or Paperchain, in which record companies can provide cash advances to creators based on number of downloads, etc.

Services catering to specific industries can offer targeted products to their customer base. We have mentioned several—Aspiration, Daylight, and more—already in this book. The neobank Nerve is another, built to serve musicians, and including several features built to meet the specific challenges of today's music industry.

Jonathan Larsen, chief innovation officer of Ping An, sums up the impact on embedded finance across traditional businesses best when he says:

> What has changed is that digital has upended the distribution models for so many businesses, providing less expensive and more convenient shortcuts. I think that what's really going on here is that what used to define industries, overwhelmingly in many cases for consumers, was the physical distribution channels that inevitably came with the business and the products. You used to go to

Tower Records to buy your vinyl and then your CDs, right? You used to go to Blockbuster Video. You used to go wherever you went for your bookshops. It could have been the corner store, it could have been Barnes & Noble, And you used to go to a movie theater to see most of the films that you consume. And we probably still do some version of a number of those things. But clearly, that's the minority, and all of those services have been digitized and they're all able to be consumed through a set of devices that we now all own that are cost-effective and are pretty much ubiquitous and end-running the traditional distribution channels and infrastructure. I think integrated digital providers, and Ping An certainly aspires to be among those, have been able to redefine the industry boundaries by bringing together value propositions in a powerful way.

Telecom

The telecommunications industry is no exception to the challenges faced by other industries. The telecommunications operator Telefonica was one of the first to make a move into financial services in Europe with its O2 banking proposition launch in Germany, supported by Fidor. This banking proposition, powered with fintech Fidor's banking platform and banking license, was offered to all Telefonica's mobile customers based in Germany. This effort by brands like Telefonica to offer banking services to customers was the first attempt at reconciling the experience of lifestyle and banking, ultimately leading to the inception and growth of embedded finance, and its limitless opportunities. Telefonica and other telcos have been looking into leveraging the opportunities provided by financial services to increase customer loyalty and lifetime value, by offering banking services to their massive audiences.

As we will discuss later in this book, telcos played a huge role in bringing banking to underserved populations with no credit history by enabling people to prove their creditworthiness through the payment of their phone bill. M-Pesa is a prime example of a fintech who leveraged this, as we will see.

WHERE DO WE GO FROM HERE?

Embedded finance requires the cooperation of several parties: a bank or regulated entity to create the basic product, a fintech service to act as a conduit, and a consumer-facing retailer to manage the user experience. Additionally, the technology and regulation must be aligned to allow the necessary interactions, and crucially, the end customer must be ready and willing to buy a financial product in a nontraditional context. All of these pieces are in place, and in the next chapter we will look at them one by one, paying special attention to the phenomenon known as Banking-as-a-Service, a necessary underpinning to embedded finance whereby bank offerings can be offered individually in context-specific settings. But the most important point is that, as shown by the myriad of examples in both the offline and online world throughout this chapter, the time is now to begin implementing embedded finance.

Summary

Despite tremendous growth in digital transactions, most commerce still takes place in the offline world. With closed-loop payment cards, Buy Now, Pay Later, invisible transactions, and more, there is rapid innovation in embedded finance in the world of brick-and-mortar retail. Any company that is consumer-facing can benefit from offering financial services.

- In an increasingly connected world, the touchpoints between brands and consumers are potentially limitless, and so is any customer touchpoint.
- Brands are offering new ways of delivering convenience to customers through the distribution of contextual financial services, such as cashierless checkout and instant credit.
- Industries as diverse as healthcare, media, and transportation all have opportunities in embedded finance.

NOTES

1. https://www.statista.com/statistics/1257230/european-consumers-that-shop-online-and-offline-each-week/ Accessed December 8, 2021.
2. https://www.inc.com/justin-bariso/starbucks-devised-a-brilliant-plan-to-borrow-money-from-customers-without-getting-anybody-angry.html Accessed January 14, 2022.
3. https://www.frbsf.org/cash/publications/fed-notes/2019/june/2019-findings-from-the-diary-of-consumer-payment-choice/ Accessed January 14, 2022.
4. https://www.americanbanker.com/payments/opinion/invisible-payments-bring-visible-benefits-and-risks Accessed October 23, 2021.
5. https://www.forbes.com/sites/matthewharris/2021/10/22/a-complete-revolution/?sh=47d7e6d3f3a1 Accessed January 15, 2022.
6. http://files.constantcontact.com/30ddbc6b001/713f63a1-9353-4a51-97ad-1e4b0aa3af11.pdf Accessed October 25, 2021.
7. https://blog.cfte.education/we-tried-to-break-the-amazon-fresh-system-and-guess-what-happened/ Accessed November 30, 2021.
8. https://arstechnica.com/information-technology/2020/02/amazon-made-a-bigger-camera-spying-store-so-we-tried-to-steal-its-fruit/ Accessed January 15, 2022.
9. https://www.digitalcommerce360.com/2019/04/05/amazon-go-may-face-competition-for-checkout-free-stores-in-europe/ Accessed January 16, 2022.
10. https://news.crunchbase.com/news/checkout-free-shopping-its-bigger-than-you-think/ Accessed January 14, 2022.

11. https://www.pymnts.com/buy-now-pay-later/2021/new-filings-show-missed-payments-are-on-the-rise-at-bnpl-firms/ Accessed January 16, 2022.

12. https://twitter.com/arampell/status/1435692958179753985?s=20 Accessed October 25, 2021.

13. https://www.affirm.com/business/blog/affirm-whisker-drive-more-sales Accessed January 14, 2022.

14. https://www.creditkarma.com/insights/i/buy-now-pay-later-missed-payments Accessed January 15, 2022.

15. https://www.volpe.dot.gov/news/how-much-time-do-americans-spend-behind-wheel Accessed November 1, 2021.

16. https://www.pennlive.com/news/2020/07/pa-turnpike-raising-tolls-again-in-2021-those-without-e-zpass-will-pay-much-more.html Accessed January 15, 2022.

17. https://www.manchestereveningnews.co.uk/sport/football/football-news/manchester-united-fans-news-latest-16771943 Accessed January 15, 2022.

18. https://voicebot.ai/2020/06/02/alexa-bill-payment-in-india-now-on-android-app/ Accessed January 15, 2022.

19. https://www.newyorker.com/culture/culture-desk/the-horror-of-amazons-new-dash-button Accessed November 1, 2021.

20. https://www.simon-torrance.com/blog/EmbeddedFinance1 Accessed January 15, 2022.

21. https://www.statista.com/topics/3382/insurance-market-in-europe/#dossierKeyfigures Accessed January 11, 2022.

22. https://www.qover.com/blog/embedded-insurance-supporting-revolut-clients-in-their-everyday-lives Accessed January 11, 2022.

23. https://www.nytimes.com/2021/07/20/upshot/medical-debt-americans-medicaid.html Accessed January 15, 2022.

24. https://www.hellowalnut.com/ Accessed January 15, 2022.

CHAPTER FIVE

THE RIGHT INGREDIENTS ARE NOW IN PLACE

W e have seen how embedded finance benefits consumers in the online and offline world and how embedded finance makes good business sense. We have also seen how customer expectations have evolved alongside technological advances that make now the right time for embedded finance to make its presence felt every day on a global basis.

Over the past few years, a combination of factors have brought tech companies, financial services providers, regulatory authorities, and consumers, exactly where they needed to be to seize the embedded finance opportunity.

The technology is in place. Through the use of APIs, Open Banking, Banking-as-a-Service, and artificial intelligence, the infrastructure is there to move to the next level.

Regulatory authorities are ready. Financial services companies report to an array of regulators, and each agency has different priorities. Consensus around innovation has emerged, and regulators are open to seeing more use cases as long as they serve the customer's interest. Regulators are now making an effort to reach out to fintech companies and understand their role in the ecosystem.

Financial services providers are ready. Banks can deliver sophisticated services by API, though not all banks (nor all APIs) are created equal. As their distribution model changes, banks will need to seek new sources of revenue, and interact with their customers in different ways. Banking-as-a-Service has matured and banks are exploring new revenue streams and reaching new customers with embedded offerings. Banks are embracing partnerships and building new models to meet customer demand. Some leading-edge banks are already here. More banks will follow.

Fintechs are ready. They have the agility to innovate and the tech talent to iterate quickly as they are constantly seeking to improve the customer experience, they have loyal customers, and they possess data they can leverage to deploy offers in context.

Let's now have a closer look at how those different stakeholders will support the growth of embedded finance.

THE TECHNOLOGY: KEY PIECES ENABLING BRANDS

Technology has been transforming the delivery system of financial products since the dawn of civilization, but the change is happening with dizzying rapidity today. The right pieces have moved into position today to make embedded finance work for your company and your customers. What are those pieces?

Artificial Intelligence

Artificial intelligence, also known as AI, is a term used to describe software that anticipates consumer needs and reacts intelligently to consumer choices. AI is strongly correlated with pattern recognition, and operates behind the scenes across the digital world to keep consumers and their data safe by identifying and stopping bad actors. AI and predictive analytics are not new. Machines were created at Bell Labs in New Jersey in the early 1950s that could predict human behavior with 65% accuracy. These machines, metal boxes as large as modern microwave ovens, used only 2 bytes of storage, or 0.0000000018 of one gigabyte.[1] Today, predictive analytics or AI has grown considerably in complexity as computer power has increased, and so has data collection.

If paired with the proper data, AI can make highly accurate guesses about customer intentions. Deployed properly, this can boost the bottom line while also delighting customers.

Not all use cases of AI result in a happy customer. AI also runs the risk of irritating or offending customers, even if the guesses the software makes are correct. The classic case of AI overreach in the retail world was the megastore Target, which used software that determined customers buying a certain combination of items were likely to be pregnant, and made offers appropriate to this situation. Imagine being the father of a teenage daughter and receiving a personal offer for discounts on diapers and baby bottles? It is easy to see how even a correct guess here might not please the recipient of such offers, or their parents, and feel like an overstep and violation of privacy. Data management is a thorny issue that must take regulations and social concerns into account. Fast-moving technology outruns both social norms and compliance.

Mobile Computing and Digital Onboarding

The use of mobile computing has grown so swiftly that two decades after it first gained popularity it is now ubiquitous, in every corner of the globe. Mobile banking may have connected nearly everyone in the world, but much of the world still lacks access to the financial tools that can lift them out of poverty. Close to 80% of the world's adults own a smartphone, and a further 10% own feature phones.[2] By 2025, it is believed that 70% of the world will do its computing solely on mobile devices. Paired with digital onboarding, mobile ubiquity means customers and businesses can connect at any time and any place.

Digital onboarding sounds simpler than it is in practice. Authenticating customers is a difficult business. A certain amount of data must be collected, but if too much is asked for, many customers will not complete the process, a behavior commonly referred to as abandonment. Convenience is one of the top priorities of every customer, and when it becomes inconvenient to sign up for a service with pages and pages of requests or questions, customers will look elsewhere, as there are often other options available.

As the world becomes more and more global and people move for new jobs or to be closer to family, their digital onboarding gets more complex when the customer's account involves multiple countries. Regulators have played an active role here and smoothed the way for customers to safely identify themselves in a number of contexts, and AI plays an important role in aiding the companies by performing checks against fraud and malfeasance. While complicated, digital onboarding is imperative for a seamless customer experience. Companies that primarily deliver services digitally but do not offer entirely digital onboarding will face severe challenges in customer acquisition.

APIs

APIs, also known as application programming interfaces, allow two different pieces of software to communicate and exchange data. In a way, APIs fulfill the early promise of the internet, connecting everything and everyone. They were first introduced to the mainstream by Salesforce in 2000 and have been the reason behind the possible rise of fintech since the 2010s, with many fintechs leveraging the services of banks through APIs and repurposing them in a new way with a new value proposition to their end customers.[3] On the surface, customers think they are only interacting with said fintech, but on the backend, nine times out of ten there is a traditional bank offering the core capabilities through their API. APIs allow your bank account or payment credentials to connect anywhere, and securely transmit data in order to make a payment or take out a loan. APIs are the reason a generation is growing up that may never need to physically handle money, visit a financial institution or even to some extent, have a primary banking app if they uniquely rely on invisible payments and embedded finance for their day-to-day needs and wealth management propositions for their savings. APIs enable customers to access multiple services with a single click. They allow businesses to open online with a single line of code pasted into their website.

APIs are simultaneously growing more sophisticated, from the perspective of developers, and simpler, from the perspective of users. They are everywhere, seamlessly connecting services to meet customer needs across the internet, allowing not only the mega banks with billion-dollar tech budgets and hundreds of developers but small banks and credit unions as well to offer their services through APIs.

Two of the most important developments entirely based on API technology that play a vital role in developing compelling embedded finance propositions are Open Banking and BaaS. These concepts at times get confused and even people in the industry mistakenly use them interchangeably, but there are a few key differences between the two.

Open Banking

Open Banking allows customers to transport their data or credentials safely, initiate payments from their bank account directly from third-party applications without having to log into their bank account, and allows applications to be built around banking data and services. One key item to note here and one of the real values of Open Banking, is that this is always with the customer's consent.

Open Banking implementation thus far is in the early days in terms of opportunities. Helen Child, founder of Open Banking Excellence (OBE), shares, "Consumer awareness and adoption will rapidly accelerate innovation of use cases beyond aggregation and payments. It will enable building consumer centric products and services, where banking becomes invisible." In a recent marketing sizing report Accenture forecast the Open Banking addressable market in the next three years as $418 billion.[4]

While early, in Europe, Open Banking is already showing traction. Helen shares:

> In 2018, the UK created the "blueprint" for Open Banking, and as of January 2022, just celebrated its fourth anniversary with over 4 million users. The leading use case in the UK is HMRC, Her Majesty's Revenue Collection, processing £2.6 billion of transitions. The UK market is advancing rapidly with new standards such as Variable Recurring Payments (VRP), NatWest being the first in the market with this game-changing payments enhancement.

Open Banking is in a highly embryonic state in the US today, but is far more developed in the UK and Europe. It is changing how customers view, manage, and access their money, build budgets and prepare their taxes, obtain loans, open accounts, and make payments. It is helping consumers better understand their holistic financial situation today and in the future while enhancing their experience with the fintech propositions they already use.

The use cases for Open Banking are quite vast. Probably the most popular use case centers around account aggregation. Account aggregation involves utilizing APIs to allow people to get an overview of their accounts. One of the most successful account aggregators globally is a company called Plaid. As of 2021, Plaid is a fintech company that is used by more than 4,500 companies to connect you to other third-party financial applications without directly sharing your login information. You may have utilized Plaid to apply for a personal loan, an auto loan, pay a contractor, open up a digital bank account, etc. Another such example of a company that fits into the account aggregation space is Tink out of Europe. With more than 3,400 banks and institutions integrated, a presence in 18 markets, and 10,000 developers using their platform, Tink claims to have built "Europe's most robust Open Banking platform – with the broadest, deepest connectivity and powerful services that create value out of the financial data" and provides the ability to instantly verify account ownership or verify income in real time on top of access to business and personal financial transaction data.[5]

The next use case for Open Banking, which saw great popularity in the late 2010s, centers around personal financial management, also known as PFM. PFM software allows you to see your entire financial life in one place to then make informed decisions about spending, saving, and investing. Have you ever wanted to know how much money you spent across all of your credit cards this month or how much you spent this quarter on takeout food? Plenty of fintechs focusing in the PFM space allow this desire to become a reality. Two of the most popular companies in this space are Mint (sold to Intuit and boasting over 15 million users as of April 2021) and Personal Capital (sold to Empower for over $1 billion in 2020) but there are plenty of others in the space from Every Dollar to Moneydance.[6] Needless to say, there is a strong desire for people to budget and track expenses, plan for the future, and set goals, and no shortage of options to help them get there. Some of the more sophisticated PFM offerings also incorporate the ability to track subscriptions, allowing users to monitor how and where they are spending money on a recurring basis. They also make it easy to cancel any subscriptions you no longer need. There are criticisms of PFM, that it doesn't reach the people who need it most, but with machine learning and additional data inputs, there's no denying PFM can powerfully aid those who choose to use it.

As previously outlined, the BNPL movement and the ability to receive instant credit approval are two of the best examples of Open Banking in action. Before Open Banking, lenders would have to put together multiple pieces of data from a potential customer and the decision could take days or weeks, with a chance that the customer is no longer interested in the loan. Through Open Banking, lenders can now get an almost real-time overview of a potential customer's credit history, and provide decisions in minutes or even seconds while the customer waits. Some of the biggest players in this space are Affirm in the US (public as of 2021), Klarna in Europe (last valued at $46 billion as of fall 2021), and many others from GoCardless, Splitit, Quadpay, and more.[7]

Another use case of Open Banking centers around opening new accounts digitally. Many of the biggest neobanks in the world take advantage of the enhanced capabilities of online account opening but many traditional players take advantage of these services as well. One of the most important aspects of online account opening centers around Know Your Customer, better known as KYC. Essentially, KYC provides all the necessary components to confirm your identity. Yet again, there are a myriad of players in this space that have gained much traction over the years with some of the biggest being Onfido (with over 1,500 customers as of 2019), Socure (valued at $4.5 billion as of November 2021), Jumio, Trulioo, and many others tackling different part of identity verification like Alloy.

While the use cases for Open Banking are vast and there are similarities across geographies, interoperability is the critical component for global success. Helen shares a helpful analogy:

> Currently each country creates individual API standards that are not instantly compatible with the rest of the world. A good analogy here to describe the current state of play would be the electrical plug sockets, with each country having their own standards. And as we all know when traveling to a different country, we need an adaptor for our electrical appliances to work. A common set of global standards would provide global interoperability.

Banking-as-a-Service

Banking-as-a-Service, most commonly referred to as BaaS, is an end-to-end process that ensures the overall execution of a financial service provided digitally. It can take on a few forms but, typically, people think of it as a model in which licensed banks integrate their banking services directly into the products of other nonbank businesses.

To understand BaaS as it is today and how it has become the main pillar of embedded finance propositions, we need to go back to the early days of its inception. As we have seen earlier in the book, neobank propositions were launched around 10 years ago. This was made possible by the arrival of APIs in fintech—which were required to connect to banks to access and distribute financial services in a new way, the fintech way—and by the arrival of BaaS providers such as Bankable and the late Wirecard, which enabled the launch of prepaid card-based propositions for retail and small and medium enterprises, or SMEs, for users in a matter of weeks. This was a revolution, enabling banking innovation at a pace never seen so far.

Neobanks and fintechs were the first type of customers served by BaaS providers. Shortly after, some banks launched their own separate digital banking propositions, with the support of BaaS providers, in an effort to catch up with those new propositions, launch in new geographies, or reach out to new target segments especially the younger demographics like millennials or Generation Z.

The banks that chose to launch a digital bank themselves took a variety of paths. NatWest launched their digital bank for businesses called Mettle with the support of the digital finance consultancy 11:FS.[8] Other banks chose to outsource such projects to the likes of Fidor (now part of Sopra Banking Software) or others.[9] Fidor in particular played a prominent role in Europe and beyond and was behind the ADIB Bank community-based digital proposition.[10] There are many other large players who are gaining traction, including Bankable who supported ABN Amro's Moneyou development by adding current accounts and payments to their savings bank proposition, and BPC who is powering the launch of Tinkoff Bank in the Philippines.[11]

While BaaS first developed in Europe and gained very strong traction in the US in the past years, it hasn't developed in China in the same way as in the West. Yassine Regragui, fintech specialist and expert on China, explains that the core business of the likes of nonbanking apps such as Alipay and WeChat is technology. While they rely on banks to offer loans or to do the KYC, because one cannot use Alipay or WeChat without having a bank card—linking those apps to one's bank—they are technology companies. For this reason, they have developed everything in-house and are providing their technologies to other wallets, in Southeast Asia in particular, where they have partnered with many wallets to enable them, thanks to their white-label technology, to speed up the payment processes to offer value-added services such as lifestyle services. Until now, there hasn't been any BaaS model because fintechs and other businesses typically go through the Alipay or the WeChat Pay onboarding process rapidly without the need for another third-party provider to build their service.

Regragui believes that BaaS may appear at some point in China because they will be interested in looking into it and potentially finding new use cases for it in a context where the number of Chinese fintech is growing at a very fast pace. Lately, many new players have developed their own payment solutions, including Douyin, TikTok's name on its native soil, and Baidu, the Chinese Google, which now offers financial services too. The current trend is for further nonbanking solutions to develop their own infrastructures, but we see collaboration with banks increasing. Newcomers will have the choice to collaborate with these tech companies, with banks, or both.

With a market opportunity in the trillions, it isn't surprising to see the multitude of companies entering the BaaS landscape. We would go as far as to say that BaaS is at the very beginning of its journey and the competition in the field is still very low, as many providers focus on specific use cases that others do not support. Also, while some BaaS providers have initially launched a one-size-fits-all proposition, more and more players are entering the market to solve the challenges for specific customer segments. We will walk through detailed examples of BaaS in practice both by traditional players, the banks, and nontraditional players later in this chapter, but, first, we must address a key pillar in true embedded finance success: regulation.

THE ROLE OF THE REGULATORS

Regulators are key contributors in enabling how financial services are reaching customers. As laws develop around Open Banking and easing rules for fintech participation in global financial systems, market participants have been emboldened to innovate. In 2020, Visa announced its intention to buy the fintech Plaid, whose APIs allow third parties to connect to bank accounts. Regulators quashed this deal when they decided it was not in the best interest of customers or the open market. Mastercard's copycat deal with Finicity, a smaller competitor to Plaid, was allowed to go through and the acquisition of Tink, the European competitor of Plaid, by Visa is still pending as of early 2022.[12] Generally speaking, regulators have supported initiatives that open up consumer choice and financial inclusion, which means embedded finance should continue to enjoy support from the world's regulatory regimes.

Few businesses flourish without regulatory and government support, or at least benign neglect. Tram Anh Nguyen, co-founder of the Center for Finance, Technology and Entrepreneurship (CFTE), a company whose mission is to empower people in the finance industry and equip them with the skills and knowledge needed to create the financial world of the future, believes that unlocking the potential of embedded finance starts with an educational effort and regulators play a crucial role in the education. This effort will aim at helping all companies looking at implementing embedded finance to better understand what it means to be working in a regulated environment, whether they are regulated themselves or working with regulated partners. Regulation is here to protect consumers and small businesses and the more that the companies leading the future of the industry collaborate with regulators, the more quickly we can make progress.

The examples of regulatory support to fintechs and beyond across the world are not lacking.

Regulation: Europe

European regulators have led the way in easing regulations to open up the market and support consumer choice. Payment Service Directive 1 (PSD1) allowed nonbank players to carry out financial transactions and required transparency around fees for services. It also helped define the single Euro payment area to facilitate payments across international borders. This directive launched in 2011. In 2015, a revised directive, PSD2, allowed payments services companies to access account information held at banks.

The EU also drives innovation with passporting, which allows a company registered in one Eurozone country to do business across the region. This lowers barriers to doing business across the entire region and compares advantageously to the US, in which money service businesses or MSBs are required to register with each and every state. This can take years and cost millions of dollars, an obvious barrier to innovation as well as consumer choice.

Passporting is a great asset to multinational companies, which can incorporate in a country with friendly local laws such as Lithuania, and use that as a jumping-off point to larger economies within the zone. Jean-Baptiste Graftieaux, CEO Europe of Bitstamp, also believes that the upcoming European Commission's Regulation of Markets in Crypto-assets (MiCA), which is a regulatory framework to provide a single licensing regime across all member states by 2024, similar to the passporting system, will enable crypto platforms to expand more easily, which ultimately will benefit embedded finance-powered crypto use cases around crypto exchanges, NFTs, and the Metaverse.

Adam Bialy, founder and CEO of Fiat Republic, considers the Payment Service Directive 2 (PSD2) to be one of the biggest developments of the past five years, as it created the framework which enabled the use cases and value chain of embedded finance. As the discussions around PSD3 are starting, he places his bet on the continued focus by the European Union on driving competition in the market. He also believes that PSD3 will provide the framework for quicker, faster, more accessible cross-border payments to all the players of the ecosystem by focusing on the upgrade of the protocols.

The UK, which is not part of the EU following Brexit, which took place in 2020, has been leading the way in fostering fintech innovation for many years. With more than 300 banks, 45 building societies, 260 EMIs, and a further 77 foreign EMIs offering services in the UK, the UK is one of the most dynamic financial services centers in the world. Thanks to its innovative and open approach to fintech, fostered by the UK Parliament mandate to promote competition and by the Financial Conduct Authority (FCA) for the implementation of this mandate, seven in ten UK citizens now use at least one fintech company to fulfill their financial services needs. In response, revenues from UK fintech rose to £11 billion in 2019—almost double from four years before and accounted for almost 10% of the global total of fintech revenues.[13]

One of the primary projects of the FCA include Project Innovate, aimed at lowering entry costs and barriers to the financial services industry. This project has since been complemented by the creation of the regulatory sandbox, in which new ideas are tested safely, with the support of the FCA, before reaching the market.

In an effort to continue to best support the UK fintech sector growth moving forward, the Chancellor asked Ron Kalifa OBE to carry out an independent review as part of its Budget 2020.[14] The recommendations of this report included:

- Ways to make the Initial Public Offerings in the UK more attractive through improvement to tech visas to ensure a continued qualified workforce for UK fintech.
- The creation of a regulatory Fintech Scalebox aimed at providing further regulatory support to growth stage fintechs.[15]
- The establishment of a National Center to promote local fintech ecosystems coordination, some of which are already under implementation, including the regulatory Fintech Scalebox with the creation of the regulatory "nursery" in 2021 aimed at providing enhanced oversight to newly authorized firms while they develop and grow used to their regulatory status.[16]

Some regulators and central banks in Europe have recognized that to foster competition, it was necessary to give fintechs access to payment rails directly, circumventing the existing system for them to have to access it through established agency banks. Until 2014, fintechs needed to contract with agency banks to access the UK Faster Payments system launched in 2008.[17] In a similar way, some European countries such as Lithuania, enable fintechs to access SEPA rails (launched in 2008 and fully rolled out in 2014) directly through the Central Bank of Lithuania while in other European countries, the easiest option to access it is through commercial banks.[18, 19] By getting direct access to the payment rails, regulated fintechs have more flexibility. The flexibility mainly comes from the fact that they don't have the need to integrate with the legacy bank infrastructure of banks but instead integrate into modern payment rails infrastructure developed in the 2010s. The result is much lower cost because the middle-man—the bank—is removed and, finally, because they don't need to manage an extra stakeholder.

Regulation: US

US regulators have started to open the doors to innovation, such as the Office of the Comptroller of the Currency's creation of fintech charters, the Federal Deposit Insurance Corporation and the Consumer Finance Protection Bureau both enacting Innovation arms, and a handful of other initiatives. Fintech charters offer access to payment rails, obviating the need to obtain licenses state by state, and have generally lighter capital requirements and the other restrictions designed to limit the risk of banks. The less rigorous regulations of these charters are designed to empower fintech companies to offer services to a broader swath of customers, but have drawn opposition from the banks and some municipalities. The US has a complicated network of regulators in the financial services space, and while there are promising signs, there is not yet broad consensus on how to handle the influx of entrants to the financial services space.

It has taken years, but fintech companies are now gaining access to the payment rails that drive the American economy, primarily the ACH (automated clearing house) network and real-time systems such as Fed-wire, from the Federal Reserve. Regulators in the US continue to look at fintech companies, particularly cryptocurrency players, with a great deal of skepticism but this is slowly changing. Obtaining access to inexpensive and speedy payment systems is a key part of enabling the launch of embedded finance propositions at scale and low cost.

Regulation: Asia

In China, the regulators have also taken a proactive approach to foster fintech innovation. Yassine Regragui mentions a handful of important regulatory-driven initiatives that are supporting fintech innovation while ensuring the protection of their users:

- **Microloans**. Two years ago, during the IPO of Ant Group, the regulator decided to regulate microloans to avoid a subprime crisis that would have come from the fact that many people could access them on both Alipay and WeChat, and as a result subscribe to many of them, and to ensure that not only people with high credit scores would be able to widen the gap between social classes. To do so, they gave more weight to the banks by imposing that 70% of microloans are provided by banks and the remaining 30% by Ant Group and other microloan providers.
- **Creating an antitrust law**. Over the past 20 years, a big share of innovation came from Alibaba and Tencent and the Chinese regulator wanted to ensure that competition is fostered so that innovation relies not only on those two players.
- **Data**. While China was not part of the General Data Protection Regulation (GDPR), the Chinese regulator wanted to put in place data policies in China, allowing Chinese companies to be ready when they expand globally.

- **Central Bank Digital Currency**. A central bank digital currency, or CBDC, has been developed in China and is already boasting 100 million users across the country. Widespread adoption will depend on when the infrastructure is deemed fully tested and ready by the Chinese government.

In Singapore, the Monetary Authority of Singapore (MAS), is seeking to accommodate new companies and encourage the building of new businesses and widening of consumer choice. The MAS even offers funding and mentorship for companies building in the island nation, encouraging the best and brightest from around the world to move to Singapore and build their fintech business there. In 2018, in partnership with the World Bank Group's International Finance Corporation (IFC) and the ASEAN Bankers Association, MAS launched APIX which they refer to as the world's first cross-border, open-architecture Global FinTech Marketplace and Sandbox platform aimed at increasing collaboration between fintech and traditional financial institutions, to drive digital transformation and financial inclusion across the Asia-Pacific.[20]

In 2019, MAS also announced that it would issue up to two digital full bank licenses (DFB) and three digital wholesale bank licenses (DWB), on top of the existing digital banks established under MAS's existing internet banking framework, in an attempt to liberalize the financial services industry.[21] The selected candidates, which are expected to go operational in 2022, include the Grab-Singtel consortium and tech giant Sea for the two digital full bank licenses and Ant Group as a consortium comprising Greenland Financial Holdings, Linklogis Hong Kong, and Beijing Co-operative Equity Investment Fund Management for the digital wholesale bank licenses.[22]

In the summer of 2021, Ravi Menon, managing director of MAS, spoke out in support of the decentralization of finance away from its traditional core.[23] Embedded finance, he noted in a June 2021 report, offers "the prospect of more efficient, more affordable, more inclusive financial services." And consequently, "Regulatory frameworks will need to become more modular and agile." But more operators in the space also opens up more potential vectors for fraud, Menon noted.

BaaS: THROUGH THE LENS OF A BANK

What does the infrastructure of the future look like? It will build on where we are today with BaaS, though it is sold as a "one-stop shop" and there are a lot of opportunities for it, there remain many plugs on the backend, resulting in numerous potential points of failure that make the true scale quite challenging.

Who addresses this issue? One option could be for the banks to really own this. Not the banks in general terms, but perhaps a select group of banks who invest the right talent, time, and resources in being the absolute best at this. A glimpse of this was seen with the blockchain consortia such as that organized by R3 in the mid-2010s. The banks that would undergo this will need to prioritize making the solution generic and evolve their KYC (know your customer), their credit criteria, and their overall onboarding process in general so that they are the partner of choice for any technology company who is interested. While they aren't there yet, there are a handful of industry-leading banks that are starting down this path.

BaaS: US Banks' Early Success

One example of a large bank that has made significant traction is Goldman Sachs, who, as Matt Harris, partner at Bain Capital says: "has invested the most dramatically in this. The Apple partnership they have now works well but it wasn't a generic solution that Apple took advantage of, it was a custom solution built for Apple." Barclays, BBVA, Standard Chartered, and Westpac have started down this path as well along with a few of the other banks.

Case Study: Goldman Sachs

Goldman Sachs is one of the largest investment banks in the world. It has several client-facing divisions, including the investment banking division, global markets, asset management, and consumer and wealth management. Transaction banking is part of the investment banking division, which generated net revenues of about $9.4 billion in 2020, 24% growth over the previous year.

Recently, Goldman Sachs has launched businesses from the ground up including Marcus, its consumer banking offering, and TxB, its transaction banking platform, which marks Goldman Sachs' entrance into the BaaS space.

Eduardo Vergara, managing director and global head of Transaction Banking Product and Sales at Goldman Sachs, explains:

> When we started thinking about this, we looked at the market and saw that while fintechs had started to disrupt the consumer space and small business space, the commercial and transaction banking space was ripe for disruption. That's because it's harder to scale a startup focused on the large corporate space. You need a large balance sheet; you need relations with large corporates. And when we spoke to our clients, we heard a lot of dissatisfaction with the existing offerings and the lack of innovation in the large corporate transaction banking space. The banks in this space all built their technology systems and their platforms in the 80s and 90s, based on 80s and 90s technology. The big advantage that we had is that we didn't have any of that legacy infrastructure because we had never played in the space.

Goldman Sachs built the TxB platform from scratch with a technology stack fully hosted in the cloud. The platform is API-first, offers real-time transfers, supports multiple payment rails, but also has the advantage of coming with a strong balance sheet, relationships with large corporates, and services that meet the needs of those types of companies.

Eduardo continues, "The other thing that was unique about what we built is everything was built API-first. Not only did we build the next generation transaction bank platform, but we also built the next generation BaaS platform enabled by those same APIs."

When it comes to building the platform, the TxB team spent months talking to treasurers from about 300 corporate clients to understand their pain points with existing solutions, understand how to solve them, and define their Minimum Valuable Product, the exact same way a fintech would do. They went through MVP iterations based on the early feedback they were getting from their customers and then rolled it out to their large corporate customers, leveraging Goldman Sachs' unparalleled network.

Eduardo also believes that one of the reasons for the success of TxB is that it was set up as a standalone business within the investment banking division. He says, "TxB is very much set up as a startup. We are now 500 people, including more than 400 engineers. We have our own product team, our own engineering team sitting next to each other, working in sprints."

When describing the use cases that the TxB platform supports, Eduardo says:

> There are generally two flavors of collaborations. One is BaaS where we will enable platforms that serve SMEs to build financial services or to expand the financial services they offer, leveraging our APIs, building on top of our platform. This includes software companies that want to expand into payments. It could be a fintech that is already offering financial services and wants to expand what they do. Our platform is just a set of building blocks that enable our partners to offer financial services for their own clients.

The other kind of collaboration that we've launched is with software companies that large corporates would use to embed our services in their front end. We want to be channel agnostic and if there's software that some corporates are already using, we want to make it very easy to use our financial services without having to log on into a different system.

When asked about traction, Eduardo explains that less than two years after announcing the launch of TxB on Goldman Sachs Investor Day in February 2020, the TxB division has already hit the five-year goal of reaching $50 billion in deposits. The transaction banking division boasts 300 clients on the TxB platform, and has announced joint collaborations with the likes of American Express, Stripe, and Fiserv. The platform is live in the US and the UK, and constantly expanding.

BaaS Is Not Just for the Big Banks

While there are some great examples of BaaS in practice at the big banks, we have seen good traction with smaller banks, particularly the BIN sponsor banks like Cross River Bank and Metropolitan Bank. (BIN means "Banking Identification Number" and is used to help clients issue credit cards, for example.) Both of these smaller banks have invested a great deal of money in technology and in their program management systems to expand their capabilities beyond being a BIN sponsor or regulatory sponsor. But how large a market opportunity is this for banks collectively? Harris feels that "it's going to be 3–4% of banks who have the wherewithal to do this." If you look at the US market, as of 2020, there are 4,377 FDIC-insured banks in the United States, using Harris's guess that would be around 130 banks in the US market.[24]

Kansas City–based NBKC has taken its own approach. It catapulted into the midst of the fintech scene by launching an accelerator, Fountain City Fintech, in 2018. Working closely with startups and helping them scale and succeed transformed the way the bank thought about its business offerings. NBKC now licenses its charter to neobanks, which means it allows nonbanks to maintain deposit accounts insured by the FDIC, and have access to the payment rails and all the trappings of being a bank. It also provides card-issuing services, and offers à la carte checking and savings accounts, as well as FBO accounts. FBO stands for "For Benefit Of," and is used to manage and pool user funds without assuming ownership of them. Legend says that the peer-to-peer payment app Venmo, now owned by PayPal, began by using one of its founders' personal bank accounts, but as the service gained popularity, this became impractical (and possibly illegal). What was needed was an FBO account to pool user funds.

Evolve Bank & Trust is an example of a bank leaning into the new ways of doing business. Evolve provides the banking services for the "banking for humans" app Dave, which went public in 2021 via a $4 billion SPAC, or special purpose acquisition company. Evolve provides banking services to a number of fintechs, despite having assets of only $400 million which, for context, doesn't rank in the top 1,500 banks in the US by asset size. The bank began as First State Bank in Parkin, Arkansas, a town with a population of just 641. In 2005, the bank changed its name to Evolve, and in 2009 it moved down the road to Memphis, Tennessee. This move placed it in a large metropolitan area and greatly improved its chances of attracting top-tier talent. Today Evolve comes up in most conversations about tech-savvy banks, and it is highly sought after for partnerships by fintechs. Fintech and BaaS have transformed the bank and this has paid off handsomely for them. As of January 2022, according to Evolve's home page, revenue has increased 74% in the past three years.[25] Sila Money is one of the fintechs that has been leveraging the services and license of Evolve Bank & Trust to serve their clients.

BaaS: European Banks' Early Success

In Europe, where Open Banking and customer ownership of financial data are stronger, many banks have taken on the primary role in BaaS. HSBC was one of the first players in the market by enabling the launch of challenger bank propositions with the retailers Mark & Spencer and John Lewis. The solution consists of white-label services provided by the retailers with a focus on credit cards, insurance, and investment services.[26]

Through its acquisition of the fintech startup Treezor in 2018, Société Générale has also put a first step in the arena, powering the likes of European unicorns, Qonto, Lydia, and Swile, and has been a strong advocate of the BaaS movement since then.[27]

Case Study: BBVA

Spanish bank BBVA often comes up in conversation around BaaS. When asked about BBVA's take on BaaS, BBVA's global head of Sustainability, Javier Rodriguez Soler stated that the bank has been implementing two key strategies since entering the space, the first a pure infrastructure play and the second, through partnerships.

On the infrastructure side, when BBVA started their BaaS strategy, the initial thought was to act as the pipes for other companies to build products on top of the BBVA core. They chose this strategy, the infrastructure play, for their US market and were known as having one of the most robust platforms in the US allowing third parties to build on their core.

In other geographies outside of the US, BBVA has taken the approach of not only being the infrastructure provider, but also being the partner to third parties that want to offer financial services to its customers. When asked about what makes an embedded finance partnership successful, like the one that BBVA completed with Uber in Mexico, Javier said there is a key characteristic, for large-scale big brand partnerships, "The bank has to be a relevant, solid, well-known bank. As was the case for BBVA in Mexico which is the market leader by a huge margin. In the partnership model, you need a bank partner with a full set of products."

The Uber model with BBVA worked well, as Uber in Mexico needed the ability to provide its drivers broad financial services, not just the ability to pay, but the larger portfolio of products available. Javier Rodríguez Soler made a reference to a handful of other very exciting examples of embedded partnerships in the works for BBVA, but at this time, those partnerships are confidential.

In terms of the impact on revenue of embedded finance, Javier shared that the impact is still quite small but in terms of transaction volume, the impact is already quite relevant. He did note that in terms of revenue, this number is "growing exponentially and that all parties involved in the partnerships are working on putting in place a profitable business model, for the bank in particular." The opportunity is clear for those offering banking services to their customers but Javier noted that, for the banks, it is still unchartered territory and it is still to be determined how profitable these types of relationships can be.

The focus for the banks and others is to ensure they have the attention of the customer. As Javier Rodriguez Soler puts it: "The ecosystem that someone creates in which the client interacts often is the one that has a big advantage in embedded finance." BBVA believes that their mobile banking app is prime territory for such a play and has invested heavily in their app over the last 12+ years.

Their investment has paid off as they are consistently recognized as the top banking app, particularly in their home country of Spain but are also on the list for countries such as Turkey. Outside of the traditional components one would expect when engaging with their banking app, it also offers additional services including the estimated value of a customer's house, recommendations for how to better manage and navigate your finances, and even advice on sustainability. BBVA's app is a prime example of what a "Super App" within financial services at the center could look like and is already on track to do so in key geographies where BBVA's mobile banking app is one of the top five most used apps on customers' phones in countries, including Spain, Mexico, Turkey, Colombia, and Peru.

ClearBank

ClearBank, launched by Nick Odgen in 2017, is the UK's first clearing bank in more than 250 years. According to Marcus Treacher, member of the board at ClearBank, the company's vision is that "the world of banking will be fully disaggregated in the near future and that elements of banking will be carried out by specialist companies like themselves that will provide a much more relevant solution than universal banks." For this reason, they exclusively focus on clearing and holding value on behalf of their customers so that they can in turn provide the best real-time payment experience to their own customers, which of course benefits the end customer as well.

In just a few years, ClearBank has become the go-to provider for UK services to the most renowned companies including Nationwide Building Society, Tide, Rapyd, Viva Wallet and Oaknorth, amongst others. Between 2019 and 2020 ClearBank has seen its revenues double from £5.3 million to £10.6 million.[28] Currently, Clearbank is working on its European expansion to support its clients across borders.

Solarisbank

Solarisbank is another interesting example relating to their BaaS strategy with a very different approach and target segments. This strategy has had a tremendous impact in empowering the rise of neobanks in Europe. Solarisbank is the enabler of unregulated fintech, enabling them to operate under its banking license, including the SME banking proposition Penta, the crypto banking proposition Nuri, and the sustainability-focused banking proposition, Tomorrow.

Solarisbank has developed a one-stop-shop solution ranging from digital banking, to cards, payments, KYC and KYB, and lending. They were established in 2015 as a part of the Berlin-based fintech company builder Finleap and officially launched in 2016, after receiving their banking license. They have raised multiple investment rounds, including raises from industry players such as Visa, BBVA, and ABN Amro, with the latest round being their Series C €60 million in 2020.

Case Study: Banking Circle

Banking Circle is another European company that is covering new ground in this space. Historically a Danish payment institution called Saxo Payments, backed by Saxo Bank, the company operated as a global transaction service provider, then was acquired by the investment fund EQT in 2018, rebranded to Banking Circle, and received a Luxembourg-based banking license in 2020.[29] Banking Circle primarily helps payment businesses, regulated marketplaces and banks, and has a very complete offering in terms of multi-currency support.

Livia Benisty, head of Business AML for Banking Circle, states: "Our solutions are powering the payments propositions of more than 200 financial institutions, enabling them to gain the geographic reach and access to the markets in which their customers want to trade. Clients currently include Stripe, Alipay, eBay, SumUp, Paysafe, PPRO and Shopify."

When asked what partnership within embedded finance Banking Circle was most excited about, they referenced their sister brand, YouLend. As Livia shared:

> The partnership between YouLend, part of the Banking Circle ecosystem and a number of technology companies such as eBay and Shopify are great examples of the real-life benefits of embedded finance. The YouLend platform enables partners to extend their value proposition by offering flexible financing products in their own branding to their merchant base with or without capital at risk. The key to the service is that it is based on the merchant's transactions and they repay as they earn, with a small fixed percentage of daily sales (typically 5–20%).

With the continuous challenges of the pandemic and beyond, entrepreneurs and small businesses are some of the hardest hit, and payment companies and ecommerce companies are especially well positioned to service them (as Tui Allen from Shopify shared with us earlier). They understand the merchants' reality through real-time data better than traditional financing providers; repayments can be linked to income; and they offer a seamless and efficient on-boarding process, simply as an add-on to the existing customer relationship. Livia continues, "Through YouLend, they can offer short-term business funding in the form of merchant cash advances and short-term loans. And because they already have access to information about a business and its revenue, it can speed up the application process, another bugbear of traditional finance routes."

BaaS: Asia and Beyond's Banks' Early Success

In Asia and beyond, some banks have also taken advantage of the opportunity of BaaS.

Standard Chartered, which is a bank headquartered in the UK with a strong presence in Asia, launched its Nexus BaaS platform in 2020. They announced they were working with a major e-commerce platform and with Sociolla, a leading personal care e-commerce platform, both based in Indonesia, to offer financial products including saving accounts, loans, and credit cards to their customers.

Kelvin Tan, Standard Chartered Ventures' lead on this project, declared that the agreement with Sociolla was going well beyond a memorandum of understanding. "It is very integrated," he said. "We want to link product design to the partner. It will be the partner that will provide our interest rates to their deposits, for example. It will be the partner that uses our balance sheet to deliver rewards in order to drive user growth."

In Australia, the second largest bank on the continent by assets under management, Westpac has taken a proactive stance when it comes to BaaS. Westpac chose the UK-based banking platform 10x Banking and AWS as partners to launch its BaaS offering in just 18 months, which is a timeframe that is quite unheard of amongst traditional banking players when deploying new technology stacks. When referring to 10x Banking, Macgregor Duncan, Westpac's general manager of Corporate & Business Development, declared: "What you've allowed us to do is create a new business model for the Westpac Group – one that enables us to embed financial services to meet the evolving needs of existing and new customers and allows our partners to create a customer experience like no other. That is unique."

So what role do partners like 10x Banking play? 10x Banking's mission, which was founded by former Barclays CEO Antony Jenkins in 2016, is to provide scalability and stability for digital inspiration of their clients. Leda Glyptis, their chief client officer, attributes the success of the deployment of their BaaS platform projects to three specific factors:

- **Make a decision**. Making the deliberate choice to select a modern and agile technology partner rather than a legacy partner.
- **MVP**. Getting the MVP, or minimum viable product right. This sounds simple but often companies, especially traditional players, can overcomplicate this. In Westpac's case, they had a use case in mind that already had strong traction. They partnered with the Buy Now, Pay Later fintech company Afterpay as they saw an appealing first customer proposition which demonstrated strong traction and solid metrics from the start.
- **Vision**. Having a very clear vision on what Westpac wanted to achieve with the launch of a BaaS offering and why. It is quite easy to get caught up in the hype of the industry or respond to a trend because a competitor is doing it. Westpac's team engaged on the project and had a deep understanding of the fundamental economics of platforms which transcended across all levels of the organization.

THE FUTURE FOR BANKS

Where does this leave the rest of the banks? One of the biggest downfalls of the financial services industry in the US is that the model was built based on geography, from state regulation to local branching laws. One of the reasons why technology has had such a large impact on the sector is because businesses are now able to become national or even global at an extremely quick pace. As Matt Harris says: "If you are basing your business model solely on state lines or zip codes, you're screwed. There are certain banks that have no reason to exist because they have 17 branches in a market of 50 and that was their strategy, and now it's irrelevant."

Our best guess? Banks will still be around but there will be fewer of them and they will continue to exist based on their competitive advantage. Instead of trying to be all things to all people, the ones that remain will specialize in one or two key things, whether it be being one of the best mortgage businesses, retail businesses, lending businesses, or even geographic advantages such as regional market share that aids you in other businesses such as retail.

This doesn't mean that banks can't offer products outside of their core capabilities, but rather, they can and should partner with fintech companies and others who themselves are best in class in this area. This goes back to the classic build, buy, partner model. What is it, at the fundamental level, that makes your business unique and what are you absolutely excellent in? This is where you should double down on your investment in terms of technology, talent, etc. and for the rest leverage others.

As chief research officer at Cornerstone Advisors, Ron Shevlin says, moving to the background in embedded finances can be a bitter pill for banks to swallow.

> It's like I keep telling them, it's simply a new distribution channel for you. Yes, your brand is not front and center. Too damn bad. Get over it. What do you want to do? Make more money or have a fancy-schmancy brand? I think your shareholders would prefer you to just make some money and provide the services. So this is the mindset that has to change on the bank side.

For the banks not willing to embrace the BaaS strategy, embedded finance can still bring a wealth of opportunities to them. Indeed, we have seen that one of the challenges created by embedded finance, which inevitably leads to invisible payments, is that payments happen without people having to think about it, which inevitably makes them think less about money and their finances. This creates an opportunity for banks to see their role evolve toward supporting their customers in making life decisions around money.

Chris Skinner believes that the role of banks is actually to inform the customer far more about the implications of how they're living their lives and what they can do to support their lifestyle. According to Chris, the future of banking is where banks actually support you and advise you during a significant moment in your life:

> Invisible or embedded payments should be used when you're just doing day-to-day transactions or day-to-day things. But when you have a major moment, like buying a house, moving home, being made redundant, or having anything else going on in your life that is unusual, that is when the bank becomes important, and should be visible and there for you. In that case, the services they provide need to cover all the needs you have at that moment in time, and use Open Banking, open APIs and banking to link across networks far more than just the local network, to create the most relevant experience for you.

BaaS: Through the Lens of Fintech

Traditional banks aren't the only ones who have taken advantage of the immense opportunity of embedded finance. Outside of the banks themselves, there are other classes of players that partake in BaaS. One group is e-money institutions that directly connect to banking partners and serve as the smart API layer distributing banking and payment and card services to the ecosystem at large—the fintechs, banks, and brands. Some of the primary players in this space across the globe include Railsbank, Modulr, Marqeta, Swan, Treezor, Weavr.io, Hubuc, and so on.

Case Study: Railsbank

The genesis of Railsbank was based on the larger challenge of just how hard it was to launch a fintech, and as such, the goal was to allow fintechs to launch a lot faster by skipping the 12 months of investment needed to build out infrastructure and focus on their core value offering. This acceleration of time allows fintechs to start signing up customers within 2–3 months through a minimal viable product or MVP. Some of Railsbank's primary fintech clients span neobanks, wealth management apps, financial planning apps, etc. Founder and CEO Nigel Verdon says that this strategy has changed now as the company reacts to consumers and consumers are getting much more obsessed about experiences. As such, Railsbank sees their customers are not only the fintech companies they started out with but also customer bases around the world like fan bases and other micro economies. When speaking of embedded finance, Nigel says:

> We call it embedded finance experiences because it's finance embedded in the existing customer wow moment or their experience of trying to do something. This will be a fundamental change in financial services. Finance becomes something that's wrapped around what the consumer is doing at that point in time, rather than forcing the consumer to go to the finance vendor.

Railsbank has a large team across the globe in three primary markets, Southeast Asia, Europe, and the US. Southeast Asia was an attractive market because fintech was still nascent when Railsbank first entered, and they have seen traction in the region ever since. In fact, one of the primary clients in the region, Singapore Life, a life insurance company, was a big inspiration for the company to dive deeper into embedded finance. Through their partnership with

Railsbank, Singapore Life uses embedded finance through their SingLife account which they provide to customers on a card allowing them to make a deposit account into an insurance product (if you look at the financials, a life insurance policy on the balance sheet of the insurance company actually looks like a deposit account). Through their SingLife card, they are engaging with their customers through their card usage on a daily basis giving Singapore Life a tremendous amount of data on their customers.

BaaS in Practice

Another batch of companies like Bankable or Sila Money focuses on a pure BaaS technology plan, while partnering with banks (Aion and Arkea for Bankable, Evolve Bank & Trust for Sila), to offer a well-rounded proposition to a myriad of players.[30]

There is no single way to do BaaS. This comes from the fact that there is a variety of BaaS customers with very diverse needs, and we are seeing more and more propositions, such as Fiat Republic's platform, dedicated to answer the needs of specific customer segments. Fiat Republic, a soon-to-be EMI regulated banking and compliance-as-a-service hybrid platform, is focusing on serving the Web3 economy. While the crypto world is experiencing a boom era, amazingly, crypto and other Web3 platforms still struggle to access traditional banking services and are often required to pay hefty risk premiums in lieu of greater assurances of compliance and security. This is the problem Fiat Republic is trying to solve. Designed to bring crypto platforms together under a Consortium to amass collective bargaining power for negotiations with banks and regulators, Fiat Republic's hybrid platform gives crypto platforms access to mainstream and local fiat rails via a single API. The company leverages data so that only the cleanest flows are processed through their banking partners, with full transparency, helping the banking partners unlock the business opportunity that Web3 flows represent. This is a win-win for the Web3 economy as a whole, crypto platforms and banks.

Beyond BaaS, offered by banks directly or fintech companies ultimately relying on banking infrastructure, a notable trend is the addition of BaaS to existing payment propositions to provide an end-to-end experience to users. Plaid, Stripe, Checkout, and others have made the move in such a direction.

Stripe

Founded: 2009

Market cap: With a valuation of $95 billion, Stripe is one of the most valuable private companies in the world.[31]

Number of employees: 48,000

Early Approach

Stripe was founded to make e-commerce easy for buyers and sellers. It operates behind the scenes and processes transactions and checks for fraud for a cut of each transaction. As an e-commerce site, you want to offer the ability for your customers to purchase your merchandise from anywhere, anytime but, one of the challenges with online purchases is serious amounts of fraud. Because Stripe's API operated with just a single line of code, it became popular with developers and spread by word of mouth.

Later, Stripe opened Atlas, a service that allows companies anywhere in the world to incorporate in the business-friendly state of Delaware. In the US, Stripe processes payments for Amazon, Uber, Google, Shopify, and this powers much of the internet economy. It is estimated that 80% of US consumers have performed transactions with Stripe, whether they know it or not. Stripe has recently launched its embedded finance product suite with Stripe Treasury, Stripe Issuing, and Stripe Capital.

Case Study: Stripe

Stripe was launched after recognizing the cost of card payments implementation was one of the most expensive ones for internet businesses. Getting started accepting card payments online took so much work and so much time that those fixed costs were holding businesses back. Stripe's original value proposition was built around the ease of implementation of card payments, and it became famous for the elegance of its API. A lot of the story over the past 10 years has been looking beyond the card transactions, into the workflows and the adjacencies around moving money online as internet businesses and platforms. As a result, Stripe now offers financial services including card issuing, bank accounts on demand, and business loans. All of this was driven by customer demand. Matt Henderson, EMEA business lead at Stripe, explains: "When we move into a new product adjacency, we're really guided by our users. We think there's a ton of opportunity in the space and that is the reason why we have launched Stripe Capital, Stripe Issuing, and Stripe Treasury, to support the full value chain of embedded finance."

Matt Henderson adds:

> When launching new products, we will frequently work with a pilot user. For Stripe Treasury, the pilot was launched with Shopify. The Shopify pilot has really helped drive further developments to Stripe Treasury, and how it works with the rest of Stripe. This approach creates a portfolio of interoperable products. The

value proposition remains the same across product lines: we want to make it incredibly easy to implement and therefore save time and resources internally for our users. This is also the case for our first three embedded finance products as well.

When asked about unexpected challenges when launching the Stripe embedded finance suite, Matt emphasizes the prioritization challenge: "We're getting requests from our clients for many different things, more things than we have time and resources to build," and the difficulty in building a strong interconnectedness between the products for the users:

> They need to be able to use the same Stripe account, the same onboarding process that they've gone through for one product to qualify them for another, they want to be able to have the same transaction data that has been used for payments to be something that informs the credit risk that would be taken into account for the capital loan. So all of these things need to interoperate really tightly and that makes building products more complex.

Matt Henderson believes that in the same way that Stripe has worked with the financial ecosystem, including card networks like Visa, MasterCard, and Amex or other payment method providers, including Klarna, the same situation will happen when it comes to embedded finance products:

> There's a particular role that these parts of the financial ecosystem are able to provide which works very well, but those players typically struggle with developer-oriented distribution that means that there's an important role for a middle layer such as Stripe, which in turn provides the building blocks required for more vertically-focused platforms to be able to create finished products. It is the model Stripe has used in payments and is likely to continue in financial services products.

What does the future of Stripe Embedded Finance look like? Matt Henderson explains:

> So with the caveat that this isn't a formal announcement and by no means imminent, we should expect that now Stripe Issuing is launched in Europe, we will be expanding it. We should also see an expansion of Stripe Treasury and Stripe Capital to Europe at some point and eventually to other parts of the world. This is the Stripe methodology: some products start with particular focus, and then we broaden the scope. When it comes to Stripe Issuing, we have gotten a lot of demand from users for the ability to issue consumer cards. On the Stripe Capital side, we could see the breadth of lending use cases expand in the future. On the international expansion front, in EMEA, Stripe is only in around 35 countries right now out of 115 in total, so we have so many more to go just with our payments product, let alone with some of these embedded finance products.

The US market is a $4 trillion credit market, which is primarily owned by four companies, Bank of America Merrill Lynch, JP Morgan Chase, Capital One, and Wells Fargo. It is well known that although these banks continue to make large investments in their technology, they still have aging tech stacks. On top of that, some are limited to the number of card programs they can launch in any given year, and they tend to cater to companies with large (one million+ customer bases).

Plaid and Stripe historically focused on one leg of the payments journey but have evolved and are now offering full stack payments solutions to their customers, demonstrating the importance of such a trend in terms of opportunity size. As introduced above, Plaid started by offering account aggregation, but grew from there into offering payment initiation and recently launched Plaid payout in the UK.

Checkout

Founded: 2012
Valuation: Checkout has recently raised more than $1 billion and is worth $40 billion, making it Europe's most valuable privately held fintech company, as of January 2022.
Number of employees: 1,100

Early Approach

Checkout.com is an API-based payment processor that accepts hundreds of payment types and currencies. Unlike Stripe, Checkout was built for the European market and its cross-border payments and multiple currencies. Since early on, Checkout was focused on enterprise clients. On top of payment processing, the company recently launched its payouts and marketplace solution and its crypto team.

Case Study: Marqeta

Marqeta, a fintech that recently went public in mid-2021, plays an active role in the BaaS ecosystem. They don't see themselves as BaaS, but rather a piece of the BaaS world. Marqeta focuses on modern card issuing and processing, which is a distinct category. Marqeta powers the automatic clearing house (ACH) and other pieces to help companies build, but their core focus is on card issuing.

Visa and MasterCard have interconnected nearly every merchant around the world, whether online or offline, making cards an important last-mile solution in global commerce. According to Jason Gardner, Marqeta's CEO, there are roughly 70 significant global card issuing and processing markets. Marqeta started in the US as it is the largest card market in the world and then expanded into Canada and eventually moved into Europe. Entering new geographies is not a simple task, especially in the highly complex world of financial services.

The expansion into new geographies is working. In Europe, at the end of Q3 2021, Marqeta said that it had doubled its customer base in the previous 12 months and seen over 340% in transaction growth year-over-year. Marqeta believes the opportunities across Europe are immense. In countries like France, Marqeta partners with the fintech unicorn Lydia that provides digital banking services with a core part of their business centering around cards. For customers who use Marqeta's platform across multiple markets, the ability to integrate once and launch everywhere is a key benefit.

It is important to Jason for his customers to have the same experience regardless of what company they work for or where it is in the world. Whether that be Europe, Australia, or the US, the relationship with Marqeta will be the same, regardless of where in the world they interact.

Jason shared: "The ability to integrate once and launch everywhere is a powerful concept that cannot be overlooked. We either support the core business or we are the core business of our customers, and that's a lot of responsibility."

THE REAL IMPACT OF EMBEDDED FINANCE

As the multitude of examples, both traditional and nontraditional show, embedded finance is already here. We have seen great strides in just a number of years and there is clear evidence that embedded finance is poised to grow rapidly in the future.

The use cases that are today in their infancy will mature and expand, and new use cases undreamed of today will emerge and gain traction. With every new technology, there are new opportunities to enhance people's lives and have a fundamental impact on society. With the birth of fintech, much was hoped for in terms of the impact on financial inclusion and banking for those underbanked and unbanked. Financial services have always favored the wealthy, and perhaps this is unavoidable. But embedded finance, because it extends the reach of services to touch virtually every adult on the planet, has the potential to be a transformative force for alleviating poverty and offering unprecedented opportunities. What opportunities does embedded finance have to truly make a difference in people's lives? What will the talent of the future look like and how should you prepare your teams? Let's explore.

Summary

The term "embedded finance" masks a great deal of complexity. Many technologies, including artificial intelligence, open banking, and mobile computing, had to reach maturity before embedded finance could be implemented. Multiple parties along the embedded finance chain have to work in concert, and consumers have to be willing to use the service in the context offered. It has been a long journey, but the technology, regulations, and customer expectations are now in place.

- Embedded finance depends on a variety of social and economic elements, as well as specific technologies, in order to develop and thrive.
- Embedded finance also requires multiple entities to work in tandem, and to have the approval of regulatory entities.

- Those multiple entities have now reached a climactic point in their development, enabling embedded finance to spread.
- Among the most important building blocks is Banking-as-a-Service, which allows banks to deploy specific banking services through new distribution channels.

NOTES

1. Poundstone, W., *Rock Break Scissors* (New York: Little, Brown & Co., 2014), p. 13.
2. https://www.bankmycell.com/blog/how-many-phones-are-in-the-world Accessed January 16, 2022.
3. https://blog.postman.com/intro-to-apis-history-of-apis/#:~:text=Salesforce%20%E2%80%93%20Salesforce%20officially%20launched%20its,did%20business%20from%20day%20one. Accessed January 3, 2022.
4. https://www.accenture.com/dk-en/insights/banking/open-banking-moving-towards-open-data-economy Accessed January 16, 2022.
5. https://tink.com/customers/rocker-finance-management/ Accessed January 3, 2022.
6. https://investorjunkie.com/reviews/mint-com/ Accessed January 2, /2022.
7. https://www.cnbc.com/2021/09/21/klarna-ceo-market-volatility-has-me-nervous-about-an-ipo.html Accessed January 2, 2022.
8. https://www.11fs.com/work/rbs-mettle Accessed January 16, 2022.
9. https://www.verdict.co.uk/mettle-digital-banking-natwest/ Accessed January 16, 2022.
10. https://businesschief.eu/corporate-finance/adib-and-fidor-offer-first-community-based-digital-bank Accessed January 16, 2022.
11. https://www.bnkbl.com/news-article/finextra-abnamro-bankable/ Accessed January 16, 2022.

12. https://tink.com/press/visa-acquires-tink/ Accessed January 3, 2022.
13. https://www.fca.org.uk/news/speeches/levelling-playing-field-innovation-service-consumers-and-market Accessed January 2, 2022.
14. https://www.gov.uk/government/publications/the-kalifa-review-of-uk-fintech Accessed January 2, 2022.
15. https://corporatefinanceinstitute.com/resources/careers/companies/top-banks-in-the-uk/#:~:text=Overview%20of%20Banks%20in%20the,of%20the%20UK%20banking%20system Accessed January 2, 2022.
16. https://www.transparency.org.uk/Image%20icontogether-in-electric-schemes-UK-e-payment-EMI-money-laundering-risk-press-release Accessed January 2, 2022.
17. https://www.fasterpayments.org.uk/sites/default/files/FPS_Payment_Access_Whitepaper.pdf Accessed January 2, 2022.
18. https://psplab.com/kb/sepa-scheme-participant-application/ Accessed January 2, 2022.
19. https://www.ecb.europa.eu/paym/integration/retail/sepa/html/index.en.html Accessed January 2, 2022.
20. https://www.mas.gov.sg/development/fintech/api-exchange Accessed January 6, 2022.
21. https://www.mas.gov.sg/regulation/Banking/digital-bank-licence Accessed January 6, 2022.
22. https://www.straitstimes.com/business/banking/mas-awards-digital-full-bank-licences-to-grab-singtel-and-sea-ant-gets-digital Accessed January 6, 2022.
23. https://www.bis.org/review/r210705i.htm Accessed January 6, 2022.
24. https://www.statista.com/statistics/184536/number-of-fdic-insured-us-commercial-bank-institutions/#:~:text=In%202020%2C%20there%20were%204%2C377,insured%20banks%20in%20the%20country. Accessed January 16, 2022.
25. https://www.getevolved.com/ Accessed January 16, 2022.
26. https://www.ft.com/content/84a41fe3-ef10-48ec-b576-51d460645b10 Accessed January 16, 2022.
27. https://www.societegenerale.lu/en/about/press-release-news/press-release-news/news/societe-generale-announces-the-acquisition-treezor-and-accelerates-its-open-innovation-strategy/ Accessed January 2, 2022.
28. https://s3.eu-west-2.amazonaws.com/document-api-images-live.ch.gov.uk/docs/RtB_vfL_NgbbAtwnXiXrL-NXg8nMdfKIR5Gp9ELVjEk/application-pdf Accessed January 17, 2022.

29. https://www.ceo-review.com/the-banking-circle-evolution/ Accessed January 3, 2022.

30. https://thepaypers.com/online-mobile-banking/bankable-aion-bank-and-vodeno-partner-to-create-a-new-banking-as-a-service-offering--1249408 Accessed January 17, 2022.

31. https://www.bloomberg.com/news/articles/2021-03-14/stripe-raises-600-million-valuing-company-at-95-billion#:~:text=Stripe%20Inc.'s%20valuation%20almost,the%20most%20valuable%20U.S.%20startup.&text=Stripe%20was%20founded%20in%202010,his%20younger%20brother%20John%2C%2030. Accessed January 15, 2022.

CHAPTER SIX

A MORE SUSTAINABLE AND EQUAL WORLD

At this point it should be clear that embedded finance makes sound business sense. While still early, the numbers speak for themselves in terms of the revenue impact that embedded finance has on businesses both online and off. But does it make sense beyond the boardroom and the balance sheet? What is the larger impact on the world and society as a whole?

This chapter will look more closely at the human element as leaders think about their teams, the talent of the future, and, more broadly, their impact on the world. Specifically, we will discuss how embedded finance fosters financial inclusion among consumers and broader society while supporting key initiatives like sustainability.

DATA AS A FORCE FOR GOOD

One of the promises of fintech, as it emerged from the financial crisis of 2008–2009 that left so many families reeling, was that it would help all people have access to financial services in a way that resonated with them. By improving their financial health, by reducing friction and speeding up access to money, by reducing transaction costs and providing more ways to budget and save, fintech was supposed to make customers' lives better.

What does financial inclusion really mean at scale and in practice? Financial inclusion means that people and businesses have access to affordable services to help them improve their financial lives. Embedded finance, by dramatically altering and expanding where and how customers touch financial opportunities, will deliver the most dramatic increase of financial inclusion in history. As Sanjib Kalita, founder of Guppy and editor-in-chief of Money20/20 says:

> It's a shift from efficiency to resiliency. What we are seeing around the world is that consumers are one paycheck away from financial ruin. What we are getting is consumers that are built up to be efficient but they're very non-resilient. With the new things coming into play, I can see a change in terms of our own consumer financial supply chains and looking at it from a greater sense of resilience rather than just efficiency.

Though fintech has opened some doors, improving customers' lives has not happened nearly as much as expected and large portions of the global population remain underbanked or still unbanked. There are a myriad of approaches for how to go about solving such a large-scale challenge. One such approach of applying embedded finance is through a much-discussed trend: cryptocurrency. Advocates of cryptocurrency believe decentralization will lead to the democratization of finance and ultimately, financial inclusion. This is what Brian Armstrong, CEO and founder of public company Coinbase, detailed in his 10-year vision for the company. A recent report by Crypto.com found that crypto users in the world grew from 65 million in May 2020 to 221 million in July 2021, close to 4x growth, showing the strong traction cryptocurrencies are enjoying, and embedded finance has played a role in its adoption, as we have already seen in this book.[1]

The shift toward digital currencies is seen throughout the world, including China. The benefits offered by the Chinese central bank digital currency (Chinese CBDC), which is already strong with 100 million users, are seen when it comes to financial inclusion. As the system and currency are offered by the Chinese state, it will ensure a widespread adoption among retailers, supporting those who cannot use Alipay, WeChat, or even cash. In terms of usage, it will remain similar to what Chinese people are used to with their payment apps and QR codes.

The author and commentator on digital financial services, Dave Birch, notes that the industry is just beginning to understand how embedded finance might work, and how its applications are broader than many realize. "People shouldn't think of embedded finance as just being about payments," Birch said. "There's a lot more to it. A lot of it is about data and providing the right data to support decision making at the right time."

Embedded finance's ability to offer greater visibility and insight into personal finances can help improve financial health. Birch said:

> People are beginning to talk about the transition from open banking to open finance. You see the emergence of what some people label, I think quite reasonably, the financial health narrative. This is about taking a bigger picture of the consumer, having access to the

consumer's finances in order to deliver them a better overall level of financial health. I think that's a very helpful narrative for the next generation of services. Embedded finance is huge. It's going to get better. It's not just about payments, it's about a lot more than that.

Indeed, embedded finance has the opportunity to bring broader financial health and inclusion to the world far beyond fintech or crypto alone because it has revolutionized the delivery system for financial services. While the problem for most underserved people across the globe can be quite complex when you get into the details, at the highest level, it can be simplified to access. For companies large and small, they already have a history with the customer and therefore, should be better able to bring financial services to meet the specific needs of historically underserved groups.

In speaking about how embedded finance impacts financial inclusion, Nigel Verdon, founder and CEO of Railsbank, believes that the impact will be huge. As he says: "Once you deconstruct a product into digital and you've got the mechanism for distribution, then you can find products or micro products when people need them. The byproduct of this is financial inclusion."

ACCESS TO CREDIT

Economic growth is quite a complex topic and varies by region but across the globe, access to credit is one of the most significant issues for members of developing economies, and one of the best ways for societies to develop healthy middle classes, which are the engines of economic growth. One of the struggles has been that developing economies typically lack the credit reporting infrastructure to properly price and underwrite loans. Outside of the infrastructure, the other primary challenge for growth lies in the thin or nonexistent credit profiles of individuals and small businesses.

Credit is one of the biggest areas where embedded finance can have an impact. We have already seen this play out in markets across the world, and there are many geographies that are in desperate need of moving from unbanked to banked. But markets that are considered more evolved from a financial services perspective, such as the US, still have a great deal of opportunity for growth. According to research done by the Federal Deposit Insurance Corporation, in 2019, there were roughly 7 million people that were "unbanked," meaning that no one in the household had a checking or savings account at a bank or credit union.[2] In the same timeframe they found that roughly 55 million people were underbanked, meaning they have a bank account but also used an alternative financial service product.[3]

That is not a small number—one in every five adults in the US qualifies as underbanked. This portion of the population is using alternative methods to traditional banks and credit unions. These include methods such as money orders, check-cashing services, or loans from various sources like pawn shops, auto title loans, or payday loans, all of which may have exorbitant fees attached to them. As Zach Pettet, host of the podcast "For Fintech's Sake" and content director for Money20/20 put it: "The embedding of financial products across the lives of humans is actually going to give data that will improve our ability to score, do underwriting, etc. We have seen this play out in other markets, so I hope that the US is that way too."

So often throughout the last 20 years, we have heard different industry leaders referring to their businesses above all else as data companies. Banking has been no exception, with banks, ranging from megabanks like Citibank to the community banks, being brought into the conversation. The key to the challenge outlined above around credit in many ways is fixed by data, which is why embedded finance becomes such an interesting value proposition. This is true not only for the companies who now have the right information to better offer products and services to their customers with the goal of expanding margins, but also for the end consumer or small business who wouldn't have typically been offered banking services before.

Eduardo Vergara, managing director and global head of Transaction Banking Product and Sales at Goldman Sachs, believes that by enabling fintech and tech platforms to provide financial services to the consumer and SME segments, embedded finance democratizes financial services by making them more accessible, putting pressure on margins due to the commoditization of those services, which ultimately benefits consumers and creates greater financial inclusion. Eduardo mentions that companies launching embedded finance propositions can leverage additional sources of data and therefore offer additional credit opportunities to businesses that they might not have been able to access with their traditional banking provider. This ultimately benefits the business itself, enabling it to borrow to support its growth, but also the economy and the employment rate ultimately.

THE IMPACT ON SMALL BUSINESSES

This data-first strategy doesn't just lie with fintech startups but also large brands such as the likes of Shopify. By using data effectively, Shopify is able to simplify the qualification process, provide funding to merchants a lot faster, while also offering more innovative repayment options. As a result, as of October 2021, Shopify has already offered $2.7 billion in funding through Shopify Capital. This data play is a "win-win-win" strategy as Tui Allen, product director at Shopify, shared with us earlier where everyone wins—from Shopify, their merchants, and the end customers.

Matt Henderson, EMEA business lead at Stripe, explains that its lending product for embedded finance, Stripe Capital, is a product with significant societal impact. In 2021, total loans to small businesses in the US were 40% lower than in 2008. Part of the reason why is that the traditional banks were struggling with being able to serve particular use cases and small businesses efficiently.

Henderson says:

If you were a plumber and you're great at your trade and you're getting a lot of bookings online, as with trading apps and so on, you've got fantastic reviews. And as a way to expand your small one-person business, you're thinking about hiring someone. Now, if you go to a traditional bank, all they can review as part of their decision protocol is your trading history, which is consistent with that of a sole trader. It's hard for banks to make a decision if they're using criteria that are based on a whole small business ecosystem rather than you specifically. Now, if you are a plumber, then the source for the loan application is actually a platform like Housecall Pro, which is a tradesperson platform that uses Stripe. The ratings are native to that platform which means that they can have confidence that the ratings are authentic. They can see from their own data that the ratings correlate with the ability for success in the future. They can then use a different sort of insight about a potential customer and do so in a scalable, automated way to make a loan decision for this plumber that then enables them to hire an extra person. Across the tens of thousands of small business loans that Stripe Capital has offered already, the revenue growth of the small businesses that have taken Stripe Capital loans shows that they on average have grown 114% faster than equivalent small businesses that haven't taken a Stripe Capital loan. It's really an amazing contrast of how such services impact these small businesses and the livelihoods of people.

Matt Henderson shared that we still have a long way to go. He says:

Most businesses, even online ones, are only selling to customers in 20 to 30 countries, some of them even less. It is a real eye-opener for realizing how much opportunity that's holding back. One of the most motivating things to work for companies like Stripe is the degree to which the infrastructure we build is used by large companies and small companies alike. This is lowering the barriers to entry for small businesses.

He continues:

Some of Paystack's users, our African subsidiary, weren't previously able to sell to customers on the other side of the city, let alone to people in other countries. The more you create a platform of capabilities that enables each user to really access the full platform in a way that is near-instant and straightforward, it creates so much economic opportunity. And even though it's simpler to understand it from a payments perspective, it's actually extremely true of the embedded finance capabilities as well, because imagine how small business loans are down in the US and the opportunity that it creates for embedded finance businesses. Imagine what that is like in Nigeria or in Indonesia or many other parts of the world where the loan options to a small business are often the loan shop next door or the local bank that says no to anybody that's smaller than a huge business.

Matt Henderson believes that embedded finance can create the same sorts of opportunities that we are starting to see in some countries now in the rest of the world, both domestically and on a cross-border basis. "I think you will see this dramatic creation of economic opportunity for people around the world, which is just a hugely impactful thing for us to be working on."

FINANCIAL INCLUSION IN THE GLOBAL SOUTH

The Global South's recent history is marred by exploitation—material, cultural, and financial—by North America and Europe, and many regions never developed sophisticated or universal banking systems. For much of the twentieth century, this meant these nations offered little or no credit to their citizens, which hindered the growth of the middle class and the development of healthy businesses.

This also meant that the transformation brought by mobile phones in the twenty-first century was greater and brought more profound change, especially true in geographies dominated by islands like Indonesia which made access to cellular networks particularly challenging. The mobile phone became the key component in the way to do things. Suddenly a suite of offerings was potentially available and located in the pocket of most adults. In these regions of the world, fintech arrived at the same time as formal banking for the majority of the population, and from bank branches to paper checks and most of the trappings of the twentieth century, these banking norms were leapfrogged where mobile payments and mobile banking became routine.

The mobile phone has created the opportunity for near-universal access, allowing people without bank accounts to send money, as well as more complex examples like the use of the device itself as a means for employment. Over the years, there have been a variety of startups that have focused on just this. One example is from a startup in Indonesia where unemployed women used their mobile prepaid phones to sell and exchange tickets, a big market in the country, and make money off the margin. This income can be $5/day, but that extra continuous income can help lift families out of poverty and it has been shown that it lowers spousal physical abuse rates as women are active contributors to the finances of the family and therefore more empowered. There are dozens of examples like this that are encouraging to look to for the future, and embedded finance has the opportunity to be a key pillar making it happen. The explosion of creativity and innovation that results from this is yet to be fully realized.

And there is more good news. According to the Global Findex database, funded by the Bill and Melinda Gates Foundation, financial inclusion, one of the most effective means of fighting poverty, is on the rise globally.[4] More than 1.2 billion adults have obtained a financial services account since 2011, and the percentage of adults living in extreme poverty is now below 10%, down from more than 33% in 1988. This is even more astonishing when we consider that the population of the world is now nearly 8 billion, up from 5 billion in 1988, and most of that increase has been in the developing world.

While we are on the right path, significant challenges remain in the way, including kleptocratic and corrupt governments, ineffective (or overbearing) regulatory structures, and more, but the companies and solutions coming out of this environment will take on problems in new and different ways than those envisioned in the developed world.

This is already happening in key geographies such as with fintech startups like Destacame, originating in Chile. Referred to on their LinkedIn page as the "free online financial management platform with the mission of improving financial inclusion and health in Latin America," Destacame started with the simple challenge of how to utilize the data of a consumer that already exists but that banks or lenders aren't currently using.[5] One of the first pieces of data they used was utility bills as it is commonplace that every home in Chile pays for this. Destacame has since expanded into other data points and other bills and now offers a suite of products that puts the consumer in control, allowing them to manage their financial life. The products include past-due debt repayment, consumer loans, credit cards, savings, and other financial health tools. This methodology of a data-first approach to improve the life of consumers is working and as of Q4 2021, according to their LinkedIn page, Destacame served more than "2.2 million users and collaborates with more than 40 financial institutions," specifically targeting unbanked segments of the population in Chile, Mexico, and beyond. It is fair to say that this approach is working.

Let's take an example from Vietnam. A farmer is likely not going to have a full life insurance policy for his family. In Southeast Asia the data typically required for underwriting such a policy is scarce, and consequently insurers are cautious about who they give policies to. Through embedded finance, however, this same farmer could have a micro life policy covering specific aspects of what he is doing, such as working with cooperatives around his seed purchases. The seed purchase itself could have some amount of life insurance embedded into it. As described before, the same way that the insurance companies' balance sheet looks like a deposit account, the farmer could buy in and out of his insurance policy. As Nigel Verdon, CEO of Railsbank, puts it: "Embedded finance is democratizing financial services because by nature it can deconstruct financial products into core components that can be distributed at micro levels. Financial services can be brought down to a size that is suitable for inclusion." The possibilities are endless.

One of the most iconic stories of embedded finance playing out globally comes out of Africa. M-Pesa is a system of value exchange launched in Kenya in 2005 by a telecom provider, Safaricom. The system allowed users to send money from phone to phone, and to cash out through a system of agents, which were brick-and-mortar retail locations. Today M-Pesa allows not just peer-to-peer and consumer-to-business payments, but credit and savings options as well, and operates in multiple countries in Africa and beyond. It is an entire financial system, all located in mobile phones, and not just smartphones. M-Pesa works just as well on inexpensive and widely available feature phones (Figure 6.1).

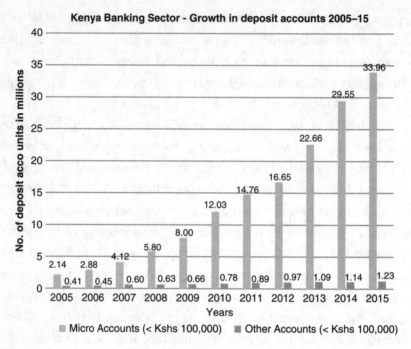

Kenya Banking Sector - Growth in deposit accounts 2005–15

Figure 6.1 In 10 years, M-Pesa facilitated the creation of more than 30 million deposit accounts.

Source: Njuguna Ndung'u 2017 / Blavatnik School of Government

The M-Pesa service was intentionally launched with financial inclusion in mind, and required the cooperation of the banking sector and the government to operate. But the reason it worked was because the mobile phone service provider already had near-universal access to the customer, because phone penetration was widespread. The banks' and even the government's opportunities to reach such a broad customer base were much more limited. The success of M-Pesa is now known around the world, and there are many similar use cases emerging from LATAM to Africa to Southeast Asia. Mobile phones are not the only means by which embedded finance will work in the developing world, but in today's world they are certainly the most important, as they are very nearly ubiquitous.

The impact and scale of fintech on the Global South are also felt among underserved customers in the West.

FINANCIAL PRODUCTS FOR THE UNDERSERVED

According to a Federal Reserve survey in 2019, nearly 40% of the US population can't afford a $400 surprise expense, meaning this is affecting large portions of populations around the world today (Figure 6.2). Let's explore what this looks like in more detail, particularly from the lens of the future workforce: the gig economy.

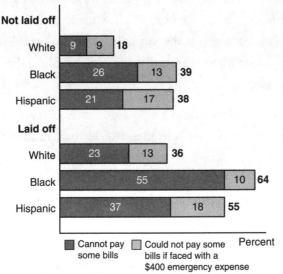

Accessible Version I Return to text

Note: Among all adults. Key identifies bars in order from left to right.

Figure 6.2 Not able to fully pay current month's bills (by layoff in prior 12 months and race/ethnicity).

Source: Federal Reserve 2021 https://www.federalreserve.gov/publications/2021-economic-well-being-of-us-households-in-2020-dealing-with-unexpected-expenses.htm

Imagine that your car breaks down because of engine trouble. Many in the world don't have enough savings to pay for the tow truck and new tire and are forced to take measures such as payday loans to pay for the essential services they need. There is a socioeconomic component to this as Zach Pettet, host of the podcast "For Fintech's Sake" and content director for Money20/20 shares:

> I used to live in a really horrible part of town and I drove a really crappy car. If you were to look at me socioeconomically without a lens on the rest of my life, you would think this is a horrible credit risk for all intents and purposes. But if you look at the next year of my life after that, things changed dramatically and I was not living in that specific area anymore. But because my driving behavior was the same, regardless of what zip code I lived in and what car I drove, I would still be able to save a few hundred dollars on car insurance. The worst part is that it was just because I was living in a specific zip code that I even had to pay that initial fee that I was saving money on.

This is primarily why companies like Root have such amazing potential to enhance the lives of their customers. At the most fundamental level, Root offers auto insurance but they use this as a wedge into the larger offerings of financial services. According to their LinkedIn profile[6], Root uses "data and technology to bring fairness and ease to car insurance." At its essence, there is a large data play here building off of driver's actions. Imagine getting insurance based on how you actually drive day in and day out. The app tracks the way that you drive, monitors things like how you turn, how quickly you brake, and so on, and therefore offers you a more favorable rate based on the quality of driver you are. Insurance acts as the wedge into getting close to their customers.

It is fair to assume that the initial target customer for a company like Root are people who are tighter on money, hence why they look to Root to help them save on auto insurance. These are likely the same people who, if on the way to work run into auto trouble, may very well likely need to take out a payday loan to pay for repairs. Because these customers already have a relationship with Root and Root has the data on them, it would make natural sense for Root, through embedded finance, to provide the loan right at the moment the problem occurs or the check engine light comes on. Because of the data that Root has, because all of the background work has already been completed from KYC (know your customer), to compliance, etc., Root is best positioned to offer this to the driver. As Pettet states: "I don't think people really think of companies like a Root as something that is interesting. But if we look ahead 10 years, we're going to say 'Oh, that's what data means to the world.' And that's what an underwriting advantage means to the world."

THE GIG ECONOMY: THE NEW WORKFORCE

We have already heard how rideshare companies like Grab and Uber are providing financial services to their drivers through their apps. Those engaged in the so-called "gig economy" are often financially vulnerable, lacking savings to draw on in emergencies, and require specialized services because they receive nontraditional payments for their labor.

The term "gig economy" has become widespread, but it risks being misunderstood. "Gig" refers to contract work, payment for specific tasks rather than hourly or salaried wages. But the term should not be taken to imply gig workers are only driving for Uber, for example, as a side job. Millions of Americans and workers worldwide depend on nontraditional work such as that in the gig economy for their primary earnings. The idea that independent non-salaried work is casual, secondary, or a side hustle is as harmful and incorrect as the notion that only teenagers or those just entering the workforce perform minimum-wage jobs.

Gig economy work has expanded rapidly in recent years, and was accelerated by the Covid pandemic that saw white-collar office workers remain safe at home while deliveries of essentials were performed by contract workers for comparatively low wages. Some estimates put gig economy participation among American workers as high as 36%.[7] The job service Upwork says there are 59 million independent workers in the US, and it expects 86 million by 2027 (see also Figure 6.3).[8]

The "creator economy" has further accelerated the boom of gig workers where people are paid for specific services and/or unique assets. While there are some in this world that have made large sums of money, many others suffer from feast or famine based on when their items sell. These workers suffer from irregular and often unpredictable pay, and often lack traditional healthcare and rely on nontraditional financial services, such as check-cashing. These workers take many shapes from drivers to on-call workers, those holding multiple jobs, and seasonal or itinerant workers.

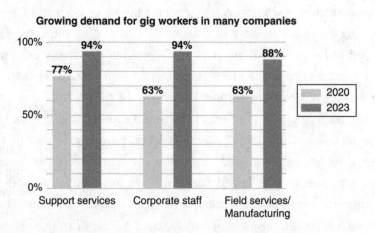

Figure 6.3   The future of the gig economy.

Source:https://www.rolandberger.com/en/Insights/Publications/The-future-of-the-gig-economy.html

They don't have time to go to a bank, and banks haven't traditionally wanted their business as their income can be unpredictable.[9]

Embedded finance is in a perfect position to assist this next generation of workers through a concept called earned wage access. The concept is simple: through earned wage access people are paid for the labor they incur that day or the project they complete or the moment their asset is sold. This is a basic but fundamental shift in society and one that has long-term impact.

Let's say, for instance, that your utility bill is due the 28th of each month, your car payment is due the 30th and your paycheck comes bimonthly, typically getting paid out the last day of the month. If you are living paycheck to paycheck, these two bills as described above come days before you receive your paycheck making it less likely you will be able to pay them on time, thus incurring late charges, and it snowballs from there.

Now imagine instead that you have the money the same day you earned it. You would then have the ability to pay on time without incurring late fees. This is not some far-off concept only applicable to the outliers of society and edge cases. Getting paid when you do the work will change people's lives.

Financial services need to be rebuilt from the ground up for nontraditional workers, from their first paycheck to filing taxes. Square recently announced it was offering free tax services to its customers. And as anyone who has been self-employed or done freelance work knows, taxes can be extremely complex, even when relatively small amounts of money are involved, and it takes a fair amount of knowledge and research to correctly identify how much to withhold throughout the year so that when tax time comes, people aren't left owing a tax bill they can't afford to pay.

Fintech has made some inroads into taking business from exploitative industries like check-cashing, which charge exorbitant fees for giving customers access to their money to offer cheaper fees to access money. While these up and comers are gaining traction, they still lack the scale to reach the many millions engaged in gig work. Embedded finance is a crucial component in opening up the true scalability of such products for society.

Uber and Grab

Uber and Grab, two companies that we have referenced a handful of times now, are key examples of embedded finance in action through the implementation of earned wage access, paying drivers salaries on the day they provide the rides as opposed to waiting until the end of week or month. These companies take this a step further by also providing loans, money for gas, etc., to their drivers, enabling them to work more and provide for their families.

Uber is a leader in offering services to its drivers through its relationship with Green Dot Bank, which offers instant access to earnings, small-dollar loans, and credit products, and also includes tax services to its drivers. Because every driver has to have an Uber app, the company can reach every single driver naturally in an experience they are already accustomed to. The company is the key here, but it can't do the work alone. We have mentioned the bank partner, and there are also startups that fit into this ecosystem, helping employers and other companies meet the specialized needs of gig workers. Providing financial services to gig workers is a win-win for employers/platforms (Figure 6.4).

With 6 in 10 people underbanked or unbanked, and 9 in 10 people lacking access to credit cards, the opportunity of driving financial inclusion in Southeast Asia is massive.[10] This opportunity became obvious very early on for Grab as they were setting up their transportation services offering. Indeed, most drivers didn't have access to basic banking services and at this time Grab was making partnerships with various banks and financial services providers to enable them to receive the payments from the drives they were completing, spend the money for their day-to-day needs, and insure themselves against accidents. Having identified this gap in the market and being conscious of their unique position, possessing the data and as a driver partner and merchant relationship owner, Grab decided to launch its own line of financial services.

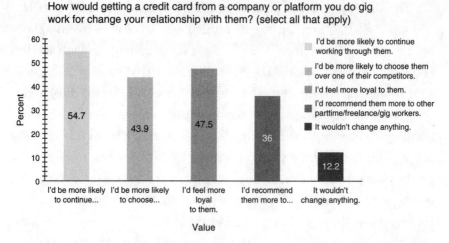

Figure 6.4 What do consumers want bond webinar.

Source: Cornerstone Advisors.

The company launched GrabPay in 2018 and then further services with micro-lending, insurance, and wealth management. They use the data they gather on their users to design products that are relevant to them and price their financial services according to the risk profile of each user, allowing them to make those services more affordable than a standard financial services provider. They also offer insurance products such as driving insurance or critical illness to those people who would not get it offered by traditional companies and adapt the premiums of those services based on the behavior of their driver partner and merchant users.

UPSKILLING TODAY'S WORKFORCE

We can't consider the social impact of embedded finance without considering how it affects current and future employment prospects.

The shifting financial landscape will create new jobs, as brands big and small will start needing experts within financial services to offset their product team. We are already beginning to see this shift take place and we know we are still in early days. According to LinkedIn, as of December 2021, Apple had roughly 30 people on their team with the word *fintech* in their title, Amazon proper (not including Amazon Web Services or other ancillary businesses) had roughly 45 people, and Microsoft had over 90 people with the word. This doesn't account for the hundreds of engineers, product designers, and marketing teams built around these offerings. At one point in time, the brightest minds were flocking into finance, then the shift went into the large tech companies, and now there is a big movement toward decentralized finance. Through embedded finance as an enabler, financial services in general will become the hot commodity again. Maybe then people will stop asking us what in the world we do for our careers:)

Fintech, with its emphasis on automation, has always had an ambivalent relationship with jobs. Yes, as the banking industry continues to undergo digital transformation, new jobs were created, attracting new types of talent. However, through automation, and the new digital world, certain roles and responsibilities will be replaced, leaving people feeling uneasy. Employment has changed dramatically as the digital economy, with its self-service and automation, has gained market share from the traditional offline economy. Skills of the present are not always skills of the future and the jobs of the future mostly don't exist yet. Some jobs requiring less traditional skill sets have been automated out of existence, while some jobs requiring high levels of specific skill are no longer relevant.[11] New skills are needed as is the new training to teach those skills. Some old-school jobs (calling all COBOL programmers) remain in high demand.

It is quite obvious that there will be many opportunities for new talent to enter the space but this movement will also require retraining many employees with outdated skills, a topic that is front and center in leaders' minds as they think about the future of work. Just because we are seeing a new trend driven by technology with financial services as the backbone, there is no reason we can't build upon the expertise of the talent within existing teams to equip them with the knowledge and skills necessary for the future. There is a big opportunity for the subsets of the working population within financial services that are at risk of their jobs being made redundant by technology to embrace the concept of embedded finance and use their background as a strength for companies outside the traditional industry (Figure 6.5).

Without a concerted effort from governments and industry leaders to reorient the workforce to be able to take on the jobs of tomorrow, many workers will be left behind. There is a big opportunity for talent to upskill and potentially change jobs better suited for the new world. In order to aid in this development, both public and private sectors need to have a clear plan for where the industry is going, about which roles will need to be upskilled

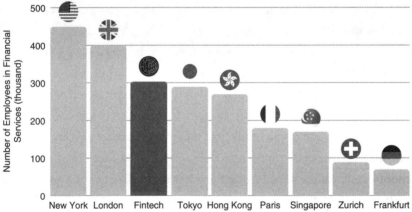

Figure 6.5 Fintech employs more people than many financial centers.

Source: CFTE 2021 https://courses.cfte.education/wp-content/uploads/2021/11/The_Fintech_Job_Report_2021_CFTE.pdf

or repurposed, and a strategy on how best to get there. This has consequences beyond merely the economic effects of unemployment and stagnating wages. The consequences have been shown to be much worse. There is strong evidence that the transforming economy and the workers it has left behind have contributed to the rise of populism and political extremism in both Europe and North America and, as such, it is imperative that we think strategically about equipping the modern-day workforce for the future.

With embedded finance, the most important jobs in banking will have to do with APIs and configuring connections to outside parties. This is nothing new to banking. After all, the ATM was first introduced 50 years ago and began the long process of reducing branch staff. The process continued with digital banking on the desktop and mobile banking. The pandemic, with its limitations on human interaction, further advanced this trend. The 2020 Financial Services Talent Strategy Report notes that bank teller roles declined more than 30% during the first year of the pandemic. And while the retention rate of bank branch staff has always been relatively low compared to other roles within banking, that doesn't mean we can't use this shift to open up a new career path for people. After all, as anyone from HR will share, it is more expensive to train a new employee than it is to retain an existing one.

The talent strategy one chooses is as varied as the company, but again, through embedded finance, there are huge opportunities as most companies offering embedded finance will need to some extent (more or less depending on how they decide to operate) internal resources skilled in fintech, banking, and regulated environments. There are several ways you can address the opportunity: upskilling internal staff, onboarding half of the staff externally and balancing the other half with internal resources, or looking purely external.

There is certainly a lot of opportunity in the future of embedded finance from a talent perspective. The question then becomes, what skills should companies look for to build out their embedded finance teams?

The Centre for Finance, Technology, and Entrepreneurship (CFTE) recently published the fintech job report, including the analysis of the more than 40,000 jobs existing in the 225 largest fintech unicorns across the globe. Tram Anh Nguyen, co-founder of CFTE, explains that even now, technology skills are already more important than finance skills and there is data to back this up. She says: "If you look at Citi, one of the largest banks in the world, it is striking that more than 50% of the current job openings are related to technology." She outlines that, on top of hard skills, soft skills, and mindset (including an entrepreneurial or, in corporate-speak, intrapreneurial spirit), and the ability to work with diverse teams in a cross-functional context, will play a key role in making those embedded finance teams successful (Figure 6.6). Her wildest guess? In 2030, most big tech companies will have an embedded finance team with very diverse backgrounds and skill sets.

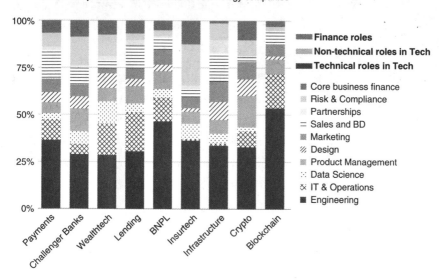

Figure 6.6 Technology is eating finance.

Source: CFTE 2021 https://courses.cfte.education/wp-content/uploads/2021/11/The_Fintech_Job_Report_2021_CFTE.pdf

When speaking with Tui Allen, product director from Shopify, she identified two key talent areas that she believed were crucial for success as embedded finance becomes more mainstream. The first area is around a team that are experts in pricing and monetization strategy. "So often, it is easy to get caught up in the excitement of offering financial services, but to really enable the win-win-win mentality, having a concrete pricing strategy is crucial," says Allen. The second area involves compliance and regulation. With a commerce platform as global as Shopify, it is imperative to have team members who are experts in the areas of compliance and regulation. As Allen puts it:

> Financial services is a very complex environment in terms of compliance and regulation. This is true regionally as well as internationally. Just keeping up with different changes in regulation. Whether it be country to country, or region to region is incredibly important. Having the right structure in place to keep a pulse on that and also to make sure that you're doing your due diligence in advance to avoid situations where you have to potentially have a bunch of rework or potentially can't enter a certain region or market.

Allen is absolutely right. This type of talent is crucial for entering the world of embedded finance and is a great opportunity for those already within financial services to branch out of their traditional roles or, on the pricing strategy side as an example, to potentially leverage talent with a data and statistical background who might not have historically leaned toward a big brand like a retailer or other.

We have seen this impact on job creation in China at a massive scale. Yassine Regragui, fintech specialist and expert on China, shares that through embedded finance in the country and the job creation induced by the development of those solutions, an estimated 40 million jobs have been created by Alibaba alone and 3 million jobs have been created by Tencent.

SUSTAINABILITY

BBVA is one of the most important financial institutions taking an active role in sustainability now and for the future. Javier Rodriguez Soler, BBVA's global head of Sustainability, believes that the bank's strategy related to sustainability is one of the two key pillars that differentiates the bank, stating: "Sustainability is a key component for the life of individuals, SMEs and big corporations." BBVA sees sustainability as much more than just an aspect of their nonprofit endeavors, but rather as core to their overall business. They believe that sustainability carries a large business opportunity, particularly in the world of ESG, also known as Environmental, Social and Corporate Governance, centered around climate change and decarbonization. In his role, Javier duly reports to the chairman for strategy and the CEO for all things business-related. The key business units across the bank in turn co-report to Javier.

BBVA is not the only financial institution taking an active role in sustainability. In 2021, at the latest COP26 conference, also known as the United Nations Climate Change Conference, the banking sector stood out as having one of the strongest levels of commitment across all sectors. According to Javier, it is believed that $7 trillion per year is going to be needed in the next two or three decades to invest in decarbonization across industries. A lot of this money will come from the public sector and off large companies' balance sheets but a significant portion of this will be channeled through banks, as it has in the past. To have the type of impact they need, BBVA believes they need to mobilize hundreds of billions themselves, and other banks agree.

What does a commitment like this actually look like? BBVA has set out a commitment with portfolio alignment in five sectors in order to reduce the relative emissions of their clients, impacting primarily large, corporate clients across coal, power sector, road transportation, cement, and steel;

and BBVA is working on a similar approach for oil and gas, aviation, ship-ping, real estate, and agriculture. Reducing the relative emissions of CO_2 or equivalent relative to the unit of energy. BBVA commits to this reduction with each client. BBVA works with each respective client to understand the plan to decarbonize; if they don't have a plan, BBVA will work with them to create a plan, and for those clients that commit, BBVA is willing to bank them further, provide larger loans, and other advantages. They take this approach on a sector-by-sector basis, and if clients don't commit in the way they are expected to, BBVA will no longer bank them.

As outlined above, for sustainability to succeed, there has to be a busi-ness opportunity behind it. Inclusive growth investing needs to be done in a way for profit. This investment benefits not only the environment but people as well. BBVA is actively doing this in geographies across the world, having a direct impact on people's lives by giving credit cards to individu-als who haven't had them in the past, opening accounts for portions of the population in Mexico and the rest of LATAM that were completely unbanked, and so on. This is a primary example about how embedded finance is good for society as a whole. As Javier puts it:

> Our presence in emerging markets, both for decarbonization where
> most of the investments are going to be needed, and the social inclu-
> sion, gives us a privileged position versus other banks in the world
> to be leading this sustainability as a business linked with embedded
> finance. Embedded finance is already including all the sustainability
> aspects. I believe we will start hearing about embedded sustainable
> finance quite soon.

Embedded finance is evident in BBVA's banking app, which also includes components around sustainability. Through the app, custom-ers can track habits including monitoring your carbon footprint through your transportation methods and your health. The goal of including such components inside BBVA's mobile app is to encourage their customers to live in a more sustainable way, emitting less CO_2.

Another point Eduardo Vergara, managing director and global head of Transaction Banking Product and Sales at Goldman Sachs, makes is that embedded finance propositions can be used to incentivize companies to improve their offerings or achieve specific goals. He mentions: "One of the things that Transaction Banking at Goldman Sachs is doing is offering an ESG deposit account for companies. Those companies are offered higher yield on these accounts when they reach their ESG goal. That's another way where we can see how some of these embedded finance offerings can have a large positive impact on society."

Yassine Regragui believes that embedded finance has been leveraged to create some environmental impacts on China as well. He states:

Ant Group launched a new feature called Ant Forest, which is a game provided by the app where the more the user uses the app or walks, the higher level of virtual energy they collect to reach certain levels. When those levels are reached, a certain number of real trees are planted in China. Around 200 million trees have been planted so far.

Tracey Davies, president of Money20/20, knows only too well the importance of this topic. She says:

At Money20/20 our goal is to reflect what the industry is thinking about but also to lead the agenda. We have always had a strong theme at the shows around fintech for good, reflecting that the industry contributes more than just profit but that the product innovation that comes from this sector can impact society and business as a force for good. Now, we have a situation that is not just about good but clearly a critical emergency for the world and one that governments, business and all of us have to lean into.

As outlined with banks like BBVA and Goldman Sachs, there have been some strong initiatives emerging, and sustainability has made its way front and center to the UN, who appointed the former Bank of England Governor Mark Carney as the Special Envoy on Climate Action and Finance. In a recent interview on the UN's website, he spoke about how private finance is increasingly aligned behind achieving net-zero greenhouse gas emissions, where emissions produced equal those removed from the atmosphere.[12]

He emphasized that with any large-scale movement, whether social or environmental, there will be cynicism and that we all want to avoid greenwash and to ensure that we are getting genuine progress and solutions. It is clear that the financial services sector can have an agenda-driving role in this if it chooses to, and choose it, it must.

THE LIMITS OF EMBEDDED FINANCE

While we are advocates for the benefits of embedded finance in the future, it is important to note some of the challenges that embedded finance will create on society and where there are potential limitations. As we have referenced numerous times, the seamless, frictionless nature of embedded finance allows users to make purchases immediately without even thinking about it. While this is a great experience from a UX perspective, the psychological nature of it is much more complex.

Embedded finance also tends to privilege convenience over privacy, as Dave Birch and others have pointed out, and this issue will be explored in more detail later in this book. Issues relating to identity fraud, privacy, and data ownership are massive, and should not be minimized just because they remain largely unknown. We will continue to learn more about each of these problems, and the education will be painful and expensive. Participants in embedded finance must be advocates for responsible use of data and identity, even if regulations and customer sentiment have not yet caught up to the dangers.

Over the holiday season, we spent time shopping for presents with a friend. In every store we entered, the friend paid for her purchases with cash. Over the course of the day, she had spent over $350 on gifts. A bit perplexed, we asked why she chose to pay cash for all the gifts; it seemed cumbersome and even a bit dangerous to carry that amount of money. Her response was simple: "Cash is tangible, I can feel it. I can see it. I know it is there and I can see it leaving my wallet. It holds me accountable." This was a profound statement. There are a myriad of reasons as to why large portions of the population are financially insecure. As a society, we, and the governing bodies around us, have the responsibility to help people make the best financial decisions for them.

One key trend playing into this over the last few years is the concept we have discussed at length, Buy Now, Pay Later (BNPL). BNPL companies are exploding around the world with many going public in 2021. Not all companies in the space can be considered equal. They serve different target markets with different spending power and purchasing needs. Optimists will point to the ability for people to purchase necessary items like repairs for their cars to get to work when they need them most. Skeptics point to the fact that BNPL offers loans to people for luxury items they don't need at the point when they are the most likely to take it, resulting in people getting into even greater debt. Credit Karma conducted a survey with consumers using BNPL in early 2021 and found that nearly 40% of all respondents who have utilized BNPL have fallen behind on payments at least once and "almost three-quarters of people with a late payment say they have seen their credit scores drop."[13]

THE QUESTION OF IDENTITY AND PRIVACY

As Ping An demonstrates, embedded finance has applications beyond offering financial services in another context. One of those is managing our identities. "Identity" is shorthand for authenticating ourselves, or proving that we actually are who we say we are. Banks have considerable expertise in this area, and with good reason. If they handed out money to the wrong person, that was a serious problem. In the old days, you would walk into the bank branch and prove your identity with a driver's license or passport, or even your signature. When accounts were opened, banks would require account holders to sign signature cards, which could be used to verify the signatures on checks and other items. As late as the 1990s and early 2000s in the US, customers were asked to sign paper forms when they wanted to move money between accounts or to another account holder.

Today identity is much more likely to be verified by digital methods, but these authentication methods can be intrusive or annoying. Dave Birch is one of the leading authorities on identity in the world. Speaking of cases where embedded finance might help consumers, Birch said:

> I think one of the simplest examples is where you're just trying to prove that you exist, that you're a person, not a bot. For a lot of online services, we can't even do that at the moment. So the services that are being provided through the embedded finance channel don't have to be transferring money and things like that. It can be other things, and I think that's underexploited at the moment.

Birch points out that the use cases don't even need to be related to finances. There may not be any money changing hands. Birch commented:

> So if I take a really simple example, if I go and sign up for an internet dating app, how does the internet dating app even know that I'm a

real person and not a bot? We're already used to situations where you go to sign up for something and you get bounced through Plaid to your bank account to sign in, not because they want you to pay anything or transfer any money, but because they want access to some other credential that can be provided through financial services.

Banks have had a stake in identity because they have a history of needing to know who you are. They also have the related task of securely storing data as well as money. Birch and a few others in financial technology have long advocated for banks to expand their services in these areas, but today when we think of ways of authenticating ourselves digitally and storing important data, most people think of Google and Apple rather than Wells Fargo or BNP Paribas.

But embedded finance goes beyond the banks to include tech companies, and Birch points out that these companies too struggle with identifying users. "Who is it that knows you're a real person?" Birch asks.

Twitter doesn't know whether I'm a real person or not. Facebook doesn't know whether I'm a real person or not, but the bank does know whether I'm a real person or not. And so those kinds of examples are maybe the more interesting areas. Like in the UK, the government was going to pass a law that you had to be over 18 to access certain kinds of services, adult services, gambling, that kind of thing. But we have no ID card, same as in America, and we have no idea who anybody is or how old they are or anything like that. So who is it that actually knows that I'm a real person, that I'm over 18? It's the bank. So it makes sense for that to become a tokenized credential that the bank can provide. There are fantastic opportunities for growth in embedded finance for financial services, payments and so on. But I also think there are really interesting opportunities for growth in other areas that are related to credentials and reputation and participation in the new economy.

Tokenization is a way to protect valuable or sensitive data, such as your name, social security number, credit card number, and so on. To do this, the sensitive data is replaced with secure data that, if intercepted or discovered by a third party, cannot be used because keys are required to unlock the information. The intercepted information is meaningless without the keys to unlock it, and even powerful computers lack the computing power to unlock tokens. Some experts argue that quantum computers, which are vastly more powerful but, as of this writing, still in their very early stages, will pose a threat to tokenization, but that day is not yet here!

Identification versus Authentication

Birch points out that though "nerdish," there is an important distinction between authentication and identification, which are often used interchangeably, and the distinction has to do with privacy.

When I buy something with my Apple Pay and I use Face ID, that's authentication. The phone is just checking. Am I on the phone? It doesn't know that I'm Dave Birch or anybody else, the phone's just checking, Is this the right person to do this? And actually, that's a very good way of doing things. It's not particularly because it's a security technology, but because it's a convenience technology. People will do it because it makes things easier and increases the overall security of the system. Biometrics as an identification technology is very tempting, and I can understand exactly why. It's the idea that, when you walk into the store and the system knows it's me, then I just go and buy the stuff I want. And then that's very tempting. But I just wonder if it just makes me uncomfortable, that level of identification. Because you can't turn it on and off. I can choose whether to turn on the loyalty program on my phone and walk in, or I can choose whether to run the supermarket app when I'm walking around the store, but I can't choose to turn my face off. It doesn't really work like that.

Birch may not be among the most enthusiastic shoppers at Amazon Fresh stores, but he points out that, in 2022 at least, most shoppers are wearing masks, which foils the technology anyway!

Chris Skinner, author, commentator, and founder of The Finanser blog, notes the common use of payments enabled by iris, face, and fingerprint recognition, specifically in China, and in the future, can happen by identifying the way you walk, which would be the ultimate act of embedded payments. We could get to the stage where we walk around, and pay for things based on just where we walk and how we walk. While there are so many ways in which technology is improving our lives, it can to some extent also become intrusive on how we live. The more identified or identifiable, the more potentially our lives become tracked and traced. So privacy versus identity is a very important issue that must be resolved.

Because embedded finance depends on identifying or at least authenticating people digitally, it favors payment methods that carry a great deal of data and context. This means that cash, which can be used anonymously and carries the least amount of data for merchants and financial services providers, is poorly suited for embedded finance. Privacy advocates often consider this aspect of cash a plus feature rather than a bug, but it also presents something of a paradox for embedded finance. As we have noted previously in this book, embedded finance is an important tool for financial inclusion and even lifting people out of poverty, and the impoverished and underserved are the most likely to be dependent on cash in their daily lives. There are often good reasons beyond privacy concerns that an individual might be cash-dependent. They may be paid in cash and lack access to an account to convert the cash to digital value. They may reside in a remote or underserved region. They may even be someone in an extreme situation such as being a political refugee, homeless, or fleeing domestic violence.

Cash use is in decline across the planet, even in countries where cash usage is common. But today there are more ways than ever to convert cash into digital value. Startups such as PayNearMe, founded in 2009, and Square's Cash App allow users to convert cash at the point of sale at brick-and-mortar locations into digital value. In Africa, Jumia allows cash payments upon delivery of orders placed digitally, and services like M-Pesa allow cash handed to physical agents to be converted to value that can be stored and spent on an account accessed by mobile phone. Ultimately it is likely that cash use will continue to decline until it remains only for specific use cases, and embedded finance by its nature is unlikely to feature prominently among those cases.

THE NEW WORLD

It is clear that embedded finance has the potential to make a fundamental impact on the world as we know it—from ESG, to financial inclusion, to the next workforce. What will the growth of embedded finance look like over the next decade? Who are the companies poised to take advantage of it? What will our everyday transactions look like when embedded finance is embroidered naturally throughout our financial lives? Let's explore the world of embedded finance in 2030.

Summary

The way people live and work is changing dramatically as a result of near-universal internet access. Through superior distribution methods, fintech has expanded access to financial services, and embedded finance will take this even further. The amplitude of the embedded finance revolution means it will impact society as a whole on multiple fronts.

- Data will be used as a way to foster financial inclusion of underbanked communities and businesses by offering them relevant financial services in a more convenient way and in the right context.
- Increasing competition on the financial services front will mean that corporations will work harder to accommodate customers and invest in initiatives for the greater good, including initiatives such as sustainability.
- The shifting financial landscape will create new jobs, as brands big and small will start needing experts within financial services to offset their product team.
- Some key challenges arising from the development of embedded finance will need to be addressed, such as identity and privacy.

NOTES

1. https://thefintechtimes.com/crypto-market-size-is-up-to-221-million-users-finds-crypto-com/ Accessed January 3, 2022.
2. https://www.fdic.gov/analysis/household-survey/index.html Accessed January 11, 2022.
3. https://www.federalreserve.gov/publications/2019-economic-well-being-of-us-households-in-2018-banking-and-credit.htm Accessed January 11, 2022.
4. https://www.worldbank.org/en/news/press-release/2018/04/19/financial-inclusion-on-the-rise-but-gaps-remain-global-findex-database-shows Accessed January 15, 2022.
5. https://www.linkedin.com/company/destacame/about/ Accessed January 15, 2022.

6. https://www.linkedin.com/company/rootinsurance/

7. https://www.smallbizgenius.net/by-the-numbers/gig-economy-statis-tics/#:~:text=About%2036%25%20of%20US%20workers%20are%20part%20of%20the%20gig%20economy.&text=If%20the%20gig%20economy%20keeps,41%25%20of%20postgraduates%20freelance. Accessed January 15, 2022.

8. https://investors.upwork.com/news-releases/news-release-details/upwork-study-finds-59-million-americans-freelancing-amid Accessed January 15, 2022.

9. https://www.rolandberger.com/en/Insights/Publications/The-future-of-the-gig-economy.html Accessed January 3, 2022.

10. https://assets.grab.com/wp-content/uploads/media/ir/investor-presentation.pdf Accessed January 3, 2022.

11. https://courses.cfte.education/fintech-job-report/?gclid=Cj0KCQiA8ICOBhDmARIsAEGI6o16HKHYzWnT1_chiiee9OAyJHHHpG28ZHqOF_oV3JxGAlkMNQxmCzkaAr2pEALw_wcB Accessed December 20, 2021.

12. https://www.un.org/en/climatechange/mark-carney-investing-net-zero-climate-solutions-creates-value-and-rewards Accessed January 13, 2022.

13. https://www.creditkarma.com/insights/i/buy-now-pay-later-missed-payments Accessed December 31, 2022.

CHAPTER SEVEN

2030: HOW EMBEDDED FINANCE TAKES OVER THE WORLD

In the early 2020s, as this book was being written, the boundaries between all of our financial lives and non-financial lives were growing weaker. By 2030, they will have disappeared entirely.

The trends we see occurring now will accelerate as the decade wears on. Banking transactions will continue to migrate to the digital world, and in-person touchpoints will decrease. Customers will still require bank accounts for many financial scenarios, but it will be just a formality, a box to check in order to fulfill a goal. The point is not to have a checking account, it is to be able to pay for experiences. The front-end communication will be handled by a trusted brand that is selling the experience the customer wants. The rest is just tools to make that happen, and is handled autonomously.

The futurist Brett King once said a bank isn't someplace to go, it's something you do. By 2030, as our financial lives become completely embedded in our everyday lives, financial activity won't even be something we do—it will simply happen—with our consent, of course.

Let's now have a closer look at what a future powered by embedded finance looks like from a consumer point of view.

A DAY IN THE LIFE, 2030 EDITION

Mia

Let's start with what a day might be like in the life of a middle-class consumer in 2030. Mia wakes up at 7 AM to the soft sound of classical music playing from the speakers in her bedroom. The shower is on, the coffee is brewing, and a holographic display shows her the balance in her bank and investment accounts, and notes price movement in a cryptocurrency she holds. She also receives health data upon awakening. Her heart rate is steady, but she is a bit dehydrated.

While she slept, her smart home system paid for the next two months' anticipated power in advance because the price is predicted to rise soon. Over the course of the day, her cloud-based wallet, boosted by machine learning and trained by Mia's preferences and risk tolerance, performs several transactions to optimize her finances, putting her in a more advantageous tax position, and earning her a few dollars here and there.

As she eats breakfast, her bills to be paid are reviewed, and her budgeting app informs her she has saved enough for next month's vacation.

She asks Alexa to book the tickets on a travel site and purchases insurance for the trip at the same time. She also asks her to book an Airbnb and purchase a prepaid entertainment pack for the city she's visiting. All of this information appears instantly in her virtual wallet and is shared with the person she is traveling with.

She has never been to a bank. She has several financial services accounts, and while she is not clear on what they are, she knows how much she pays in fees each month. But as to how the financial infrastructure behind her wallet works, she has no more need to know than she knows how her car engine works, or how the refrigerator stays cold.

When it's time for work, Mia puts on her headset and steps into the virtual office. Work takes about four hours, then she says goodbye and checks out.

Later in the day Mia gets in the car to do some shopping. Her car brings up menus from restaurants along the route in case she wants lunch. She pays for an order through the car, which is connected to her wallet. The food will be ordered just in time so that it is delivered to her when she makes it back home. When she travels along a toll road, the car pays. Because it is a high-congestion time of day, the city charges a small fee, which the car alerts Mia to, then pays, since it is not optional.

At her favorite store, Mia is identified through her facial biometric data when she enters. The store communicates with Mia's wish list, and offers items on the list that are high priority to her. One of those is a new chair that Mia has been considering. The store can offer advantageous financing on the item, but Mia is saving for something else, so her AI system turns down the offer, but will notify Mia later so she can consider it at her leisure. Meanwhile, she tries on several items of clothing then leaves with two of them. The store knows which items she chose, and debits the funds from her account as Mia walks out of the store.

When she returns home, Mia looks over her vacation plans again. She may need a new surfboard. She picks one out but the price is a bit high, considering she has spent so much on her ticket. The store offers an interest-free payment plan, and Mia gets the surfboard without having to pay anything up front. The file appears in her 3D printer and within minutes the surfboard is ready.

Over the course of the day Mia withdrew funds from her bank account multiple times, performed several currency exchanges, and invested in new assets, but she didn't have to "do" any of it. It all happened, along the lines she had previously laid out.

Mike

The next day, Mike, a rideshare driver, starts his shift. Mike also operates with a cloud-based wallet, but being in more straitened circumstances than Mia, he operates quite differently. He carries some debt, and his primary financial concern is paying it down and refinancing it.

Mike's bank account is through his rideshare platform, and he is paid instantly for his rides. He uses the income from his last ride to fill up his tank, never having to leave his car or take out his wallet. Like Mia, Mike's wallet moves funds around when it is advantageous, but unlike Mia, Mike's risk tolerance is very low because he doesn't have a lot of spare funds at his disposal.

During the course of the day, between rides, Mike gets a flat tire and pulls over. He doesn't have the funds right now to pay for a tire, but it's not an optional purchase. Without it, he can't do his job. He has several options. His employer will finance the purchase for him, or he can use financing from the auto parts store he frequents. Mike enters the tire he needs and his wallet informs him the store deal is better than his employer's, so Mike contacts them and an hour later an employee is on the scene and putting on the new tire. Mike can't afford to pay for the tire in four weekly installments, so the financing company sets up a custom arrangement for him. For only slightly more interest, Mike can pay the loan back over the course of three months. The loan is offered based on Mike's driving history and predicted income and Mike has the option to have a small amount deducted from each ride or to pay in weekly lump sums. He chooses a per ride deduction plan over three months. He doesn't want to carry the loan that far, but this arrangement allows him to continue the rest of his financial plans with minimal interference, and his flexible work arrangement gives him the option of driving for an hour more here and there to pay the loan off more quickly.

Later in the day, Mike receives an alert: his heartbeat showed a slight irregularity earlier. It may be nothing, but it should be checked out. Because his health insurance data is embedded in his wallet, the wallet can make an appointment with his doctor for next week, and order a refill of his medication. Mike opts to have it delivered by drone this evening rather than driving out of his way to pick it up today, while the drone option incurs a small fee, his virtual wallet informs him that the potential income he would lose by driving to pick up the medication is greater than the drone fee. That night when Mike gets ready for bed, his smart mattress suggests he aims to get to sleep 30 min earlier as the data from his watch shows that he sleeps better and is more productive with a slightly earlier bedtime.

WHAT ELSE CAN WE EXPECT FROM LIFE IN 2030?

Embedded finance will transform every aspect of society and business in 2030 from the way we interact with our data, to how we consume insurance products at point of context, to how we manage our health. This impact will not only be seen on consumers but on businesses as well, enabling them to make smarter decisions in real time, fostering growth.

Data

The environment will be highly interactive, with far more points of contact and data exchange than today. Walking down the street, intelligent systems will interact with your digital aura, the way your AI-powered wallet interacts with the environment. It will be preloaded with interests in order to streamline the kind of marketing that you will engage with, and reject incoming signals the user has not approved. Today we have catalogs of cookies on our web browsers, but we are not fully in control of them, and are being tracked by sites that we visited once and would rather not be associated with. Remember when you ordered a Thomas the Tank Engine toy and book set for your boss' son that one time only but have been targeted with multiple Thomas the Tank Engine ads across your digital life since? This will no longer be the case in 2030.

There will be far greater awareness of the importance of maintaining the integrity of our data. What we do, including what we now call our digital footprint, forms a rich picture of our lives and interests, and though many companies together comprise this picture, in totality, it belongs to us, just as a chef uses many ingredients to create something new and unique. The individual pieces are vital, but they are only fractions of a whole. In 2030, there will be a greater understanding of this, and just as we today maintain rights about our person and our property, the same protections will extend to the data we generate. Data has value, and companies that want to use our data to make money will need our permission, and in some cases, will need to pay us. Our data has the ability to be passive income streams for us depending on how and where we feel comfortable sharing it.

Data plays a crucial role in optimization as well. How do we enable money to work for us as it did for Mia and Mike? Not in the way that many of the wealth management platforms are focusing on but on everyday purchases and interactions? It all starts with making optimization easier and more intuitive. This is already happening where people are using a certain card on their groceries that gets them 5% cash back at grocery stores and then perhaps their airline card for when they book their travel and hotel that gives them triple the points. Can you imagine a world where this is all automated and optimized so that you don't even have to think about which card you use but rather your virtual wallet automatically uses the right card for the right transaction in the right place?

As Sanjib Kalita, founder of Guppy and editor-in-chief of Money20/20, says: "Easy optimization is key. With embedded finance and also in parallel, thinking about consumer data vaults and AML [anti-money laundering] to optimize some of that data, embedded finance could change things as far as how many options consumers can juggle at a time, or consumers don't have to juggle at all." This optimization can span beyond everyday payments into any interaction with our financial lives. Should we be refinancing our home mortgage more? How often? Is it worth the time, effort, and savings? As Matt Harris, partner at Bain Capital, says:

> We're earning less interest than we should. We have balances everywhere that are lazy and sloppy as we don't have time for the optimization equation. But software has time for it. And so as our lives become more driven by software than the negative net interest margin that we all experience—paying too much for credit, earning too little on float, etc. We're all paying too much for financial services through our passivity and having software to handle that for us is going to be amazing.

Insurance

Insurance is already undergoing transformation with digitization, but has been more resistant to change than banking. Younger and less affluent customers only purchase insurance when it is required, and insurance products often do not seem to be necessities. In other words, many people are willing to carry the risk of being uninsured unless they are required to be insured. In 2030, insurance will be available in targeted microdoses, in context, around experiences customers want. Insurance will be situation-specific, often of quite limited terms, and underwritten entirely by AI. Companies such as Hippo and Lemonade already offer sophisticated home insurance products that can be underwritten and sold in minutes with a few taps of the screen.

Health

Health insurance is an area that is a prime opportunity to continue to build out IoT to offer insurance products. Companies like Fitbit, Apple Watch, Garmin, and others are already gathering enormous amounts of health data and understand to a highly specific degree the behaviors of the people who are wearing the devices. It is only natural that then they could offer insurance products on top of this. We still have a way to go with this from a global perspective. In areas like Europe, health data is very sensitive and the regulations don't allow companies to price products depending on health risk or end user behavior. In the future, you can imagine that companies will be able to use this data to either prevent damages so that people have a better lifestyle or to gather data in case there is a disease, health crisis moment like a heart attack, or multiple comorbidities that may be present with certain individuals. This concept is already making its way into pop culture as the Showtime series, *Billions*, highlights in an episode relating to a heart attack. One of the key figures is on an exercise bike during his routine workout only to find the paramedics at his door. They have come to find out his condition, as the smart health ring on his finger noticed abnormalities and was able to prompt medical intervention, saving the character from a life-threatening heart attack.

Marketing and Advertising

Every brand in 2030 will seek to build strong relationships through direct digital contact with their loyal customers. Relationships with brands could grow intensely personal, if we allow it. People may voluntarily interact with a brand for hours at a time on a regular basis and place deep trust and affection in that brand.

Studies by the British anthropologist Robin Dunbar show that the average person can maintain 150 or so casual friendships, up to 15 close friends, and five intimate relationships. Perhaps humans can maintain five "intimate" brand relationships as well. Marketers should consider how their brand can be one of those, for thousands or even millions of people.

Through tracking of digital touch points, brands will be able to determine if they're "intimate" with a customer, close to them, or just casual friends, and adjust offerings accordingly. This will make a difference when brands are the ones offering financial products. Intimate customers will be treated differently. In the age of embedded finance, relationships matter more than ever and embedded finance will enable brands to build those relationships by wooing the customer through seamless financial and lifestyle experiences, always delivered at the point of context.

The opportunities created by embedded finance aren't true only for end consumers but also for merchants, especially around marketing and advertising. As Livia Benisty, head of Business AML at Banking Circle, predicts:

> Embedded finance will be integral in every B2B2C proposition. I am personally excited about how finance can increasingly be embedded into the user journey for specific large purchases instead of being a standalone product. For example, I expect that in 2030, merchants will be able to obtain financing when they buy online advertising from companies like Facebook and Google and only repay when their online advertising translates into real sales—compared to today where they have to take a loan separately, buy online advertising and repay, independent of whether their online advertising worked.

Sustainability and Inequality

Consumption will become more local. Unnecessary travel of our persons or products will be considered excessive. 3D printing as a means of creating consumer goods will assume vastly greater importance as far fewer manufactured goods travel on container ships from China to the world's ports. Items made of common materials will be 3D-printed on demand very close to their desired location (if not within the home itself!). Today there are already 3D printing machines that can build homes in 24 hours. They will soon routinely build every conceivable consumer product, from cars to food to custom cabinetry to artificial limbs. Today Amazon prints books on demand, while in 2030 Amazon will print just about everything on demand. You will pay for consumption not only for the products we consume, but also for their disposal. California is already imposing fees for trash collection. This will increase greatly, particularly in progressive jurisdictions. Individual responsibility for the creation of landfill or pollutants will be tracked and assigned in the hopes of reducing harm.

William Gibson's famous maxim is: "The future has already arrived. It's just not evenly distributed yet." It is worth remembering half of Gibson's maxim: The future arrives unevenly. In 2030, though the number of people living in poverty will be lower, the gap between rich and poor will still exist, and may be wider than ever before. Since at least 1895, when H. G. Wells's *The Time Machine* was published, a consistent vision of the future is that the rich have gotten still richer. One expectation of embedded finance is that it will bring more people into the financial system and provide them with the opportunity for financial success. The mass personalization allowed by digital banking, as well as the democratizing effect of digital tools, which are quite similar, no matter what your income, serves to have a flattening effect on the differing experiences of both the affluent and the struggling.

The Convergence of Online and Offline

The connection between online and offline is currently a fairly disjointed experience. When you walk into a shop to purchase a bag, they likely don't know who you are but if you visit that same shop online, they likely recognize you through cookies or site login being stored with automatic sign-in for repeat visits. If the online shop then has the ability to embed rewards and other incentives to encourage you to let them track you, the online shop can offer you a better experience while you are in their offline shop. There is a tremendous benefit for the retailer, the brand, and you, the consumer, because you get appropriate things that are directly relevant to you when you want them most providing real value.

A big part of our lives will continue to be offline and more and more in the future the two worlds will collide. Javier Soler, BBVA's head of Global Sustainability, believes that "more and more, the online and physical world become one and the same." You may use your app to call a car to pick you up and you may order your food ahead of time from your phone, but you are still physically going to the restaurant to consume your meal with a friend and discuss life. As far as banking goes, Javier states: "Our belief at BBVA is that those banks who develop the most in the online world, but at the same time have a relevant physical presence, are the future winners." While Javier sees that there is a trend in the shift to the online world, those that crack the code at mastering both will be the long-term winners.

Eduardo Vergara, managing director and global head of Transaction Banking Product and Sales at Goldman Sachs, believes that the distinction between online and offline will be increasingly blurred, with embedded finance driving this change. In particular, he mentions the Internet of Things:

I think what you're going to see is financial services being embedded into those offline experiences. Whether it's your car or your refrigerator, you'll see financial services embedded very soon. You're going to see cars paying for gas when you pull up to your gas station, or your refrigerator ordering and paying for groceries that you're running low on.

Zach Pettet, host of the podcast, "For Fintech's Sake" and content director for Money20/20, believes in the ongoing connection of the two worlds as well. Zach states:

My hope is that the digital world is informing the physical world in a way that is improving human lives, specifically meaning health, happiness, and wealth. Likely this will change our work lives so that people that want to be creators for a living, can be creators for a living and really do it in a way where they're supported with the infrastructure necessary to do that where they can think about everything necessary to do that, from soup to nuts, starting with taxes and moving from there.

There are many things to think about when imagining how the online and offline world intersect, and one key area to look at involves fraud. Today, the offline world is typically known as the safer world when it comes to fraud, especially within financial services. It is still common for people to go into a branch and open their bank account with their ID and get access to their funds and services much more quickly because they were there, in person. While you have the ability to open up an account online, many customers still feel that the level of fraud is higher, hence the plethora of companies flocking to the space focusing on identity, security, and fraud. But what if, in 10 years from now, those two worlds were flipped? As Sanjib Kalita says: "Imagine a world where people trust you more online than offline. What are the implications of that?"

The Wallet of the Future

Transactions in this future world will be frictionless and invisible, yet the pricing will be transparent. Our digital wallets will do our transacting for us, autonomously and with our permission. The busy consumer will be spared many tedious transactions, and the underserved consumer will see opportunities open up where none existed before.

Rather than carrying cash or even cards in a physical wallet, value will be stored in a digital wallet that will be our primary account. This "wallet" is actually a sophisticated piece of software that manages multiple payment accounts, loyalty programs, and perhaps manages our investments and our identities. The value held in our wallets can be traditional funds, cryptocurrency, store credit, gaming tokens, and much more. All of this value will be accessible and fungible within the wallet as users perform transactions.

In 2030, small routine transactions will be autonomous, machine-to-machine. Purchases will not require interacting with a cashier or even a website or app shopping cart. The purchase will be logged, invisibly but transparently, and your wallet will pay the merchant. This will also be the case for non-discretionary payments, such as bills. If it needs to be paid, artificial intelligence (AI) will know and do it. When approval is needed, the user will be notified. When it comes to major purchases, offers and discounts will arrive automatically, but approval will still be manual. Non-essential purchases (the fun stuff) will also largely be manual, but the potential for automation within defined parameters will be high and ubiquitous. AI will review competitive offerings and make sure your choice is the optimal one for that time and place.

What form will this AI agent take, and "where" will your wallet reside? It will not be in the personal device you carry in your bag or pocket everywhere you go. Or rather, it will not *only* be in your personal device—it will be in every device you possess, in a cloud or aura that surrounds you, or stored in many places, a capability offered by Web3, which is a new iteration of the World Wide Web that incorporates decentralization based on blockchains, that is gaining strong traction.[1,2] And there will be far more connected devices in 2030. Your home, your vehicle, even the places you visit outside the home. Your digital aura will interact with the digital presences of brands, institutions, other people, and data will be exchanged. It is analogous to the self-driving cars that will be the standard in 2030. Most interactions will be dealt with autonomously, and only occasionally will you be required to intervene in your own financial life. But these autonomous transactions will be context-rich and if you wish to look into them, there will be a great deal of detail to investigate.

Consumers in 2030 will use more financial products in a day than many of us do in a month in 2022. This is because financial products have been sliced into context-specific bites and are delivered via trusted brands at the time of need. An ecosystem of fintech companies surrounds the base financial accounts and makes them accessible to top-level, consumer-facing brands.

The typical wallet of 2030 will see money in constant flux, shifting between different currencies. The same way portfolio managers operate today, our wallets will operate in 2030. If we have too much money sitting in cash that is depreciating in value, our wallet can shift the funds over to a cryptocurrency or other asset that is more resistant to inflation. Micro investments in cryptocurrency and trading with fractional shares will happen automatically, along user-defined parameters and risk tolerances, without the user having to even think about it. The trading will not just be in traditional stocks and funds, but in shares of scarce commodities such as sneakers, classic cars, baseball cards, and of NFTs, or non-fungible tokens, which are unique and non-interchangeable units of data stored on a blockchain, a form of digital ledger. NFTs can be associated with reproducible digital files, such as photos, videos, and audio—and grant the holder the unique and undisputed ownership of the associated digital file.[3]

Beyond the view of how the wallet of 2030 operates, we could have a multitude of wallets, depending on the context we use them for. Brett King has been predicting the type of wallet we foresee in 2030 since 2010. King believes in a multitude of wallets that will not necessarily be neutral or interchangeable. We will have wallets from different companies, with different strengths, biases, and priorities. Some wallets might focus on investing, others on saving. Dave Birch, author and commentator on digital financial services, points out that some wallets could be shopping-centric, from the likes of Shopify, while others would be more investing-focused or financial-focused, from PayPal, or a bank. These wallets will come to be our new primary financial institution. If we're crypto-focused, it could be Coinbase. So while banks might fade into the background in many cases of embedded finance, in the future when our wallets are more important, banks will have more competition, but they can still claim significant mindshare by providing convenience and the right services.

The Interplay of AI and Human Decisions

Dave Birch has some thoughts on how the AI or wallet systems described above might function in practice, and that, in some ways, the future is already here. "There's some legislation in the U.K. whereby gambling companies have to check that you are safe to gamble," Birch said, noting that this would apply also to payday lenders and others who would also need to guarantee that you had the funds or means to pay back the loan.

> One obvious way to do this is by using open banking data to access your account and check that you haven't spent too much on gambling. Obviously this happens with your consent. Things like that are really a very interesting shift. So you're trying to help the consumers and support them and take care of them, but in order to

do that, you have to have a picture of what they're doing. And then you can use AI and machine learning and so on to help them make good decisions. And it's kind of a weird thing to say, but the average person, and I include myself in this, doesn't necessarily make good decisions around finances. You don't have to be dictatorial. Just the right nudging at the right time can help people to make the right decisions.

Birch is optimistic that embedded finance can be beneficial to consumers, but as with identity proving intrusive, AI too poses challenges. And when a financial services company's AI is talking to your AI-powered wallet, well, the consumer may not be part of the conversation.

I hope what embedded finance means is that you have much more informed consumers of financial services and much more sophisticated providers of financial services. You have to have the right kind of consumer protection around this, but hopefully with AI, that should be easier as well. One implication of that is that the financial products themselves will probably get a lot more complex because when you have AIs talking to AIs, if you're trying to sell me a pension, I don't understand anything about pensions. It's impossible for me to make the right choice the way legislation works at the moment. It's almost perverse that I'm even in that loop. It's like, why are you even asking me? There are rules that say you have to ask me for consent. Why? I don't know the first thing about it. I want the most super-intelligent giant pension killer robot on my side. And that means that the bank is no longer selling things to me. It's selling things to my AI.

This has profound implications for the future of marketing, according to Birch.

That's a real change in financial services, because what's the point of sponsoring the Super Bowl? My AI doesn't care about the Super Bowl. What's the point of you telling me you've got this 300-year-old brand? My AI doesn't care about your 300-year-old brand. All it cares about are the numbers, what are the returns and so on. So there are implications that go way beyond just the fact that if we get access to more people's data, if it's embedded in more services, we can nudge people to help them to make the right decision. Yes, we can. But it has implications that go beyond that because the sophistication of the products will grow as well.

And while it is simple to say that our AI-powered wallets will help us make more responsible decisions, there is a lot of nuance here. For example, sometimes we want to splurge, even if it isn't the financially optimal thing to do. We have emotional connections to products or brands and there are societal impacts on what is "cool" or "in style" that AI can't comprehend. How much control do we want to cede to systems that, while vastly more sophisticated than humans could ever be, may not understand the importance of relaxing or taking a moment for mental health?

Birch describes the idea of indulging in an expensive takeout meal. "Ordering a $60 pizza instead of a $30 pizza on a Friday night is probably not going to make that much difference to your overall financial health," he says.

> But making a really poor choice on your 401K does make a big difference to your life and your health. And that's where I feel I would need support. You think of the myriad little choices that are made through the day. Some of those are long term, some of those are short term. I can't figure all of that out. I do stupid things all the time with money. But does that mean, with an AI by my side, I would never get a $60 pizza? I don't think so. I like to think my giant killer pension robot would be a bit more tolerant.

The Future of the Web

Web3 is getting colossal attention at the moment. The reason for this is that it offers an open, trustless, and permissionless network, which, unlike the previous iterations of the Web, no single entity controls, yet everyone can trust, as every user follows the same set of rules, known as the consensus protocols. Web3 offers clear solutions to the shortcomings of the Web 2 internet. With Web3, the power shifts to the user.

"With embedded finance, consumer attention is a limiting factor but with Web3, that edge point is going to be the deciding factor. So you have the limiting factor and the deciding factor lining up to be at the edge of a decentralized small data point as opposed to a centralized large entity," says Sanjib Kalita. This means that whether you have the patience and attention to focus on the details, you will be able to have the right products at the right price point that ultimately benefit you without having to get into the nitty gritty. Kalita continues: "Whatever technology is able to organize all those endpoints is going to be even more powerful."

The momentum from the industry is all leading to one place—identity, the sovereignty of, the ownership of, and the monetization of, identity. A good execution of Web3, or what Web3 will inevitably be is that, solving for digital identity in the digital future. What does this look like in practice? Zach Pettet says:

> It is the changing of the rails and the underlying technology to enable people to have the control and liquidity of their own identity. Web3 is just going to be another layer inside of embedded finance that will allow you to transact faster, that will allow you to lend your identity or to lend social clout to something in a provable way.

The idea of lending your social clout by sharing things like your social media presence to enhance your experience by either building further validation, reducing cost, or simplifying the process is not a new concept, as we have seen its uses in early days though alternative credit scoring but one that has a long way to go.

As we have seen previously, some established crypto platforms are moving into offering one-stop-shop embedded financial services to their retail users, including loans, saving offerings, and crypto-backed cards. But in the future, what does the life of a crypto user look like in 2030? Jean-Baptiste Graftieaux, CEO Europe of Bitstamp, supports the vision that crypto users will have a one-single view of all their assets and liabilities, potentially up to their art and music NFT collection, in a similar way we have seen PayPal evolve their initial proposition to give you the ability to pay, take a loan, and hold your assets. He also believes that crypto exchanges, which are relying on embedded finance providers for their fiat needs and who are already offering embedded finance services to their users, will play the bridge between crypto, NFTs, and the Metaverse.

Adam Bialy, founder and CEO of Fiat Republic, explains that embedded finance represents the intersection of the crypto industry and traditional financial ecosystems. He believes that embedded finance acts as a protocol between them, enabling traditional finance to unlock the growth of Web3, and that is going to remain the case for at least the next 10 years.

When it comes to crypto democratization, Matt Henderson, EMEA business lead at Stripe, believes that real-world crypto use cases are coming: "We see applications such as the possibility to use stablecoins to move money from one part of the world to another. I think those use cases will be important in our future."

Fintech has evolved over time and the next evolution is one that will take decades to come to full fruition. As Matt Harris, partner at Bain Capital Ventures, says: "The next chapter is from centralization to decentralization (DeFi). The protocols that exist in DeFi create really interesting economic opportunities, they are largely unregulated and the Wild West from a user experience perspective and from a risk of loss perspective." Because of this we are likely far off for consistent use by everyone across banking and insurance. But this change is coming and Matt believes: "The first breakthrough application will be stablecoins where you have a representation that is, generally speaking, collateralized, so the risk is quite manageable. Once you've abstracted dollars away from dollars or euros or pounds sterling, you actually get real friction removal benefits from that." This is step one and "once you move people one abstraction layer away from actual fiat currency, then it's not that hard a thing to move the lending and borrowing and savings and yield and investments and ultimately, insurance. But this is going to take years."

THE VIRTUAL WORLD OF THE FUTURE

In her Coindesk article, "Web3 and the Metaverse are not the same," Annie Zhang, host of "Hello Metaverse" podcast, explains:

> The metaverse—which gets its name from the 1992 sci-fi novel *Snow Crash*—is more of a vision than a concrete reality. Many people imagine it to be a 3D immersive world that is synchronous, persistent, and unlimited in concurrent users. It is a digitally native place where we will spend the majority of our time to work, learn, play, entertain, etc. The metaverse feels vague and speculative because it is; it hasn't really taken form yet. While some technologists want to anchor the vision along the lines of Meta's Ready Player One-esque keynote presentation, the reality is the metaverse will require everyone's input and participation to truly take form. It should encompass the confluence of different iterative efforts and technological advancements and have no discrete end.[4]

Looking at the future and the Metaverse, this will certainly impact society across the globe and likely the traction will start with the younger generation, as we are already seeing. Kids and teenagers today are having active lives in these digital environments. This is done with everything from games like Fortnite, PubG, Roblox, and others but also through virtual lives where kids can have their own virtual farms, pick their vegetables, tend to the animals, and so on.

Why will this span generations? Because this version of virtual life has existed years before the sophistication we see today. In the late 1990s, there was a trend with Tamagotchi and Giga Pets, the first pocket-sized digital companion. This computerized pet was one that kids could raise and take care of—being responsible for keeping the pet alive—and kids were connected with the pet from birth to death. As this technology continually gets more advanced and cheaper, larger portions of the population will be inclined to engage.

The concept of the virtual world in many ways can also help society as a whole become one planet versus separate geographies and countries. In the physical world, we are bound by the physical limitations of our circumstances. If you are born in a small town in Alabama to a poor family, it is likely that you will not leave the United States in your adolescence, thus limiting your interaction with the cultures and people who are classically different from you. The same could be said for a child growing up in a remote village in Micronesia. But, because of the ubiquitous nature of the internet coupled with these virtual worlds, today, kids can be gaming with other kids from all over the world. In games that encourage collaboration to help achieve goals and problem solving, naturally through the process, the gamers will get to know each other on a personal level—habits, customs, vernacular, etc.

The Metaverse in Practice

Let's first explore Facebook, now known as Meta, a potential version. It could be expected that in Facebook's Metaverse, they will create it in a way that is similar to how they have behaved with their other assets to this point. They will likely want to control the hardware, the user experience, the data around the experience, and as such will likely control the economy as well. Will Facebook's Metaverse succeed? Time will tell but they certainly have the scale and network of bringing people together, so they have a good chance.

Who else might win in this future Metaverse and what could it look like? Matt Harris from Bain Capital Ventures says: "Apple probably has a legitimate shot at it. Google would be next on that list, and it falls off dramatically. Maybe Microsoft after that." Outside of these companies, there is a large opportunity for a decentralized virtual world. Matt says: "You will have all sorts of real-world economic players who need to have things like branches in the Metaverse and offer their services as it relates to payments and then over time, real substantial financial services." The companies who are already winning when it comes to providing payment opportunities within virtual gaming could certainly be key players in solving the complex payment challenges within the Metaverse as well.

Chris Skinner, author, commentator, and founder of The Finanser blog, believes that Metaverse banks and coins will have a key role to play to enable transactions in the Metaverse:

> If you're living a second life, which is what the Metaverse will be, you are going to need to have the same things that you have in your real life. And it's interesting because when Second Life came around in the 2000s, people were making thousands of dollars out of virtual property. The Metaverse is a second virtual life and in the virtual life, you'll need a virtual bank to store virtual money.

The Second Life virtual world Skinner refers to is mostly notable in financial circles today for Linden Dollars, its proprietary closed-loop currency, and the wider Linden economy, which included interest payments and taxation. By 2009, when bitcoin was born, the Linden economy made up 25% of all virtual value online.

Railsbank founder and CEO Nigel Verdon is another believer in an embedded future in the world of the Metaverse, specifically around the digital asset management side of the house, powered by blockchains where you have provenance of the digital asset. "One of the major things in the digital world will be around provenance tracking, whether that be a sword, a skin on a car, a piece of virtual real estate," he says. Razorpay is one example of a company already looking at doing this and many others are exploring as well. There are infinite possibilities, such as ownership of digital earth, or micro ownership of a valuable piece of artwork that you own in the Metaverse with the real piece of work still hanging in a museum in France. Nigel sees this as an opportunity to democratize ownership of art in a way that many have dreamed of but haven't had the right execution to this point. He leans toward the Jack Dorsey thinking on the topic saying: "The internet becomes the way that assets transfer into each other in a sort of distributed way and it's not until we have a common protocol on the internet or the Metaverse, like we had with email address and SMTP, that it will really take off."

Matt Henderson explains that when it comes to the Metaverse, Stripe might become an infrastructure provider to companies that are building tools that are operating in Metaverse-like environments. "You may have some use cases whereby a gamer may want to get some microloan to buy assets in the game. We will stop using the Metaverse term so distinctly between the internet and the metaverse, and it'll be more of a sort of blurred continuum."

And what about insurance? There are two paths that get insurance investor and founding Partner of Astorya.vc, Florian Graillot excited. The first is one that many will expect—cyber security. The second one gets much more interesting and is IT based on time. As Florian puts it: "If there is a bug in your internet connection, then that means you cannot access the Metaverse, and this could cause you all kinds of damages." Quite an interesting world to think about, getting damages because of lack of accessibility to the internet and a virtual world, which for many, may be their primary form of income in the future. Another path that insurance could potentially take in the Metaverse, is property insurance. It is very likely that there could be an insurance product for protecting your second life assets.

AN EMBEDDED REVOLUTION

We are in the midst of tremendous change in the overlapping worlds of financial services and technology. We are already able to perform actions with a few taps or clicks that a decade ago would have taken hours. This is going to continue until we won't perform financial transactions at all. They will be performed on our behalf, along parameters we have defined, and they will take place instantly, and more optimally than we could have hoped for had we done them manually. This will be possible because financial services will be distributed through an endless variety of endpoints that maximize customer convenience while also benefiting the companies teaming up to provide them.

The idea of banks and banking will change. Our vision of our financial life will change. But it is an opportunity for more companies to service customers in new and better ways, and it can help the struggling as well as the wealthy. It will be equally relevant in Shenzhen and Chicago, Sarasota and Zaragoza. It will be a revolution as profound as any in technology, and represents a huge opportunity for any company with a customer base.

As a consumer, the way you experience money will change forever as we enter an era of automatized wealth management and invisible payments in the online and offline worlds.

As a corporate executive, the question is how will you look back on this decade? How did you take advantage of it? In this book we have described the companies that have already taken up this challenge and seen early success. We hope to see your company add its name to that list and look back in 2030 on years of hard work and great prosperity.

2030 is not far away. It's time to get ready.

NOTES

1. https://en.wikipedia.org/wiki/Web3 Accessed January 9, 2022.
2. https://www.businessinsider.com/what-is-web3-internet-blockchain-cryptocurrency-web1-web2-future-2021-12?r=US&IR=T Accessed January 9, 2022.
3. ttps://en.wikipedia.org/wiki/Non-fungible_token Accessed January 9, 2022.
4. https://www.coindesk.com/layer2/2021/12/21/web-3-and-the-metaverse-are-not-the-same/ Accessed January 16, 2022.

ACKNOWLEDGMENTS

This book would not have been possible without the generous contributions of the people and companies paving the way for the future of embedded finance. Their perspectives and real-life examples provided the context necessary to bring embedded finance to life through their stories and those of their customers, painting the picture of embedded finance in practice and its impact.

We would like to say a big thank you to Tui Allen, Livia Benisty, Adam Bialy, Dave Birch, Helen Child, Tracey Davies, Jason Gardner, Leda Glyptis, Jean-Baptiste Graftieaux, Florian Graillot, Matt Harris, Matt Henderson, Michael Jackson, Sanjib Kalita, Shamir Karkal, Brett King, Jonathan Larsen, Tram Anh Nguyen, Lex Oiler, Zach Pettet, Yassine Regragui, Javier Rodriguez Soler, Ron Shevlin, Chris Skinner, Neri Tollardo, Marcus Treacher, Nigel Verdon, Eduardo Vergara, and Orlando Zayas.

And, finally, we would like to thank the amazing Bill, Samantha, and Purvi from the Wiley team for their guidance with these first-time authors as well as Jill Marsal and Philip Ryan for their support along this journey.

ABOUT
THE AUTHORS

Scarlett Sieber is chief strategy and growth officer at Money20/20, the fintech industry's largest gathering place. Scarlett is one of the industry's most sought-after speakers as a thought leader and innovator, with expertise in driving organizational change at both startups and enterprises alike across the financial services and fintech ecosystem. Scarlett has been a consultant, banker, strategist, and tech entrepreneur and has held senior executive roles in financial services, including at USAA and BBVA.

Scarlett holds a bachelor's degree in accounting from Fordham University. She currently serves as a senior advisor to NASA and is an advisory board member to Village Capital. Scarlett has been invited to speak at over 100 prestigious financial services and technology conferences around the globe. As a prominent industry influencer, Scarlett is an invited recurring contributor to *Forbes*, *The Financial Brand*, and *Huffington Post* and has been quoted in dozens of other publications, including *Yahoo Finance*, *Bloomberg*, *American Banker*, the *Chicago Tribune*, and the *Los Angeles Times*.

Sophie Guibaud is the co-founder and chief commercial and growth officer of Fiat Republic, a compliance-first banking and payments API for crypto platforms.

She has been a trailblazer of embedded finance, having spent the last 10 years designing and executing the go-to-market of BAAS and embedded finance propositions. Prior to that, she was part of the founding team of HelloFresh in the UK, and worked in investment banking and as a tech investor.

Sophie sits on the Fintech Advisory Board of PayU, the fintech arm of public company media giant and Tencent's largest shareholder, Naspers, and is an associate mentor of the University of Oxford's Said Business School Creative Destruction Lab Fintech incubator.

She has delivered speaking engagements on some of the world's largest fintech stages. For her work within the fintech industry, she has received multiple industry recognition awards, such as Standout 35 2018 and 2019 by Innovate Finance, 35 Women under 35 from *Management Today/The Telegraph* and has been named as one of the European Digital Financial Services "Power 50" by the Digital Banking Club.

INDEX